ENVIRONMENTAL CHEMISTRY:
EXPERIMENTS AND DEMONSTRATIONS

SECOND EDITION

Martin G. Ondrus
University of Wisconsin-Stout
Menomonie, WI

Wuerz Publishing Ltd.
Winnipeg, Canada

phone   (204) 453 7429
fax   (204) 453 6598
email   swuerz@wuerzpubl.mb.ca

Wuerz Publishing Ltd.
Winnipeg, Canada

**Environmental Chemistry:
Experiments and Demonstrations**
Second Edition
Martin G Ondrus

ISBN 0-920063-69-1

Printed in the United States of America

Table of Contents

Notes

†   A simple, reliable experiment.

*   Suitable for fairly large groups.

‡   Best done by small groups or independent study students, and requires specialized equipment.

Experiment   **Notes**   **Page**

Notes

†   A simple, reliable experiment.

*   Suitable for fairly large groups.

‡   Best done by small groups or independent study students, and
requires specialized equipment.

Notes

†   A simple, reliable experiment.

*   Suitable for fairly large groups.

‡   Best done by small groups or independent study students, and requires specialized equipment.

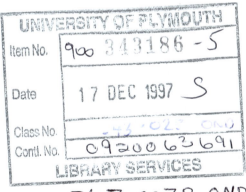

PREFACE

This lab manual is intended to be used with a laboratory notebook. The author feels that summarizing the experimental procedure, recording the data and the calculations in an orderly fashion, and discussing the results of the experiment help solidify the experimental concepts in the student's mind. The cursory report sheets included with some of the experiments should serve as a guide for setting up data and calculations in a logical fashion and for keeping notes or sample calculations. They are not meant to be handed in to the instructor.

The experiments range in length from about 1.5 hours to about 3 hours, but instrument time may, in some cases, increase the length of the experiment considerably depending on the number of students and the kind of equipment available. An ideal lab size would he relatively small at about 14 students per lab.

Several new experiments have been added to this manual since the first edition. Experiment 8, "Acidity and Alkalinity of Drinking Water", was added because these parameters are important in determining the corrosiveness and acid-neutralizing capacity of water. Experiment 12, "Molecular Models", was added to give the student an opportunity to visualize the structures of environmentally important organic compounds. Experiment 21, "Preparation and Properties of Ozone" has proven to be interesting and straightforward. We were surprised by the quality of the UV spectrum that could be obtained with a capped cylindrical 2-cm cell. Experiment 24, "Single Digestion

Procedure for Determining Phosphorus, Calcium, Magnesium, Potassium, and Nitrogen in Plant Tissue", is an analytical procedure for determining. rather quickly, the concentration of certain nutrients in environmental plant tissue samples. It has proven useful for independent-study students, and parts of it may be used as a normal student laboratory exercise. Experiment 2, "Effect of Heavy Metal Ions on the Growth of Microorganisms", has been changed considerably. It now reliably illustrates the ability of copper and mercury to kill or inhibit the growth of yeast.

At several places in this text, the instructions call for "purified water". The student may use distilled, deionized, or distilled/deionized water - but not tap water.

The demonstrations which follow Experiment 24 are several that this writer uses regularly in the lecture. They are all well known to General Chemistry instructors who use lecture demonstrations. However, these have proven particularly applicable in teaching Environmental Chemistry, a course with fewer appropriate demonstrations.

Martin G. Ondrus
1996

Copper and Arsenic in Treated Wood

General Discussion

For many years, chemicals or mixtures of chemicals have been used to treat wood in an effort to extend the lifetime of the wood under conditions which would normally accelerate deterioration. Examples of treated wood include telephone poles, fence posts, deck lumber, railroad ties, and plywood used for wood foundations. In the past, two important wood preservatives were "penta" (short for pentachlorophenol) and creosote (also known as coal tar which is obtained by heating coal and distilling off an oil). The use of pentachlorophenol has been found to contain dioxin, a highly toxic manufacturing impurity, and creosote is known to contain dozens of carcinogenic polycyclic aromatic compounds.

In recent years, wood has been pressure treated with a water solution of a green colored aqueous solution containing copper, chromium, and arsenic. This compound, called "copper chromated arsenic", is toxic to insects, bacteria, and small mammals and also retards the growth of mildew and fungus. The problem with it is that it is water soluble and can slowly leach out of treated lumber. Copper, arsenic, and chromium can also get into groundwater if spent solutions used to treat lumber are improperly disposed of. Also, burning wood treated with this compound can contaminate a large area around the burn site with toxic metal compounds. Breathing smoke or sawdust containing these metals is hazardous.

The purpose of this experiment is to use atomic absorption spectrophotometry to determine the percent by weight of copper and arsenic in a sample of exterior grade lumber which has been treated to prevent rot and mildew.

Reagents

a. **Nitric acid solution (6 N).** Prepare by diluting reagent grade 15 M nitric acid with purified water.

b. **Copper stock solution (1000 μg/mL).** Dissolve 1.0000 g of metallic copper in 50 mL of 1:1 nitric acid and dilute to a volume of 1 liter.

c. **Arsenic stock solution (1000 μg/mL).** Carefully weigh 1.3203 g of arsenious oxide (As_2O_3). Dissolve it in 25 mL of a 20% KOH solution. Neutralize the resulting solution with 20% (v/v) H_2SO_4 to a phenolphthalein endpoint. Dilute to 1 liter with 1% (v/v) H_2SO_4. Final concentration is 1000 μg/mL As.

Instrumentation

An atomic absorption spectrophotometer should be equipped with a 4-inch single-slot burner head and Cu and As hollow cathode lamps. Detection is done at 324.7 nm for copper measurements and 193.7 nm for arsenic. Deuterium background correction is recommended for the short wavelength required for arsenic determination.

Extraction with Nitric Acid

Carry this procedure out on two samples so that duplicate results may be obtained and averaged. Weigh into a 250-mL erlenmeyer flask (to the nearest milligram) approximately 1 gram of small particles (or saw dust) from a pressure treated wood sample. Use of the electronic balances will be demonstrated by the instructor. Add 50 mL of 6 N nitric acid and bring to a boil on a hot plate <u>in a hood</u>. Boil gently for 10 minutes replacing any volume lost due to evaporation with purified water from a wash bottle.

Allow the two boiled samples to cool. Filter using a vacuum filtration apparatus. Rinse the erlenmeyer flask three times with 10-mL portions of purified water, each time pouring the rinse water through the funnel so that it is added to the 50 mL of filtrate. Transfer the filtrate combined with rinses to a 250-mL volumetric flask and add purified water to the flask to bring the total volume to exactly 250 mL. Cover the flask and turn upside down several times to provide thorough mixing.

These samples will be analyzed for copper or arsenic by atomic absorption spectrophotometry. Depending on the amount of laboratory time available, it may be necessary to store these solutions along with the following standards until the next laboratory period for AA analysis. After standing for several hours or several days, the wood extract solutions may become cloudy even though they were filtered by vacuum before dilution to 250 mL. Filter about 25 mL of the solution by gravity through a piece of filter paper folded to a conical shape in a funnel. If the solution is cloudy and is not filtered, it is likely to clog the nebulizer of the atomic absorption spectrophotometer.

Preparation of Standard Solutions and Analysis

Standard solutions containing either copper or arsenic for instrument calibration are prepared in the same manner. We will use standards having concentrations of 0, 5, 10, 15, 20, and 25 µg/mL.

0 µg/mL Add 20 mL of 6 N nitric acid to a 100-mL volumetric flask and dilute to the mark with purified water.

5 µg/mL Dilute 20 mL of 6 N nitric acid, and 0.5 mL each of copper and arsenic stock 1000 µg/mL solutions to 100 mL using a 100-mL volumetric flask.

10 µg/mL Dilute 20 mL of 6 N nitric acid, and 1.0 mL each of copper and arsenic stock 1000 µg/mL solutions to 100 mL using a 100-mL volumetric flask.

15 µg/mL Dilute 20 mL of 6 N nitric acid, and 1.5 mL each of copper and arsenic stock 1000 µg/mL solutions to 100 mL using a 100-mL volumetric flask.

20 µg/mL Dilute 20 mL of 6 N nitric acid, and 2.0 mL each of copper and arsenic stock 1000 µg/mL solutions to 100 mL using a 100-mL volumetric flask.

25 µg/mL Dilute 20 mL of 6 N nitric acid, and 2.5 mL each of copper and arsenic stock 1000 µg/mL solutions to 100 mL using a 100-mL volumetric flask.

Use the standards prepared as outlined above to obtain absorbance readings using the atomic absorption spectrophotometer. A wavelength of 324.7 nm should be used for copper measurements, and 193.7 nm for arsenic (use the fuel/air mixture, slit width, and lamp current recommended by the atomic absorption spectrophotometer manufacturer). Background correction must be used for arsenic determinations. The copper concentrations used in this experiment are relatively high because copper is detected with great sensitivity. To reduce absorbance readings, it is recommended that the burner head be tilted 10° when making copper measurements. Also, use the instrument to measure the absorbance of the solutions containing copper and arsenic extracted from treated wood. Record all data on the report sheet.

Prepare standard curves for copper and arsenic by plotting the concentration of the metal on the x-axis of a piece of graph paper against absorbance on the y-axis. Draw a straight line (or smooth curve) through each set of points beginning with the origin. For each of the two samples extracted, locate the copper absorbance on the copper standard curve and the arsenic absorbance on the arsenic standard cu₁ ve. From the curve, determine the concentrations of copper and arsenic in micrograms per milliliter (μg/mL).

Calculations

Calculate the concentration (in μg/g) of metal in the original wood sample using the following equation.

$$\mu\text{g metal / g wood} = (\mu\text{g metal / mL extract}) \frac{(\text{final volume of extract})}{(\text{grams of wood})}$$

NOTE: In this and all subsequent experiments, be sure to use significant figure rules to round off calculated values to the correct number of places. If you are unsure of how to use the experimental data to decide how to round off results which are calculated from the data, talk to the instructor about it.

Waste Disposal

Stock solutions and standard solutions of heavy metals (copper and arsenic) should be disposed of in the waste heavy metal container. All other solutions may be rinsed down the drain with water.

Discussion

Consider sources of error which might have caused your final calculated concentrations to be incorrect. Some, but not all, possibilities include: (1) weighing error, (2) dilution error, (3) error in measurement of stock solution volumes, and (4) loss during extraction, filtration, or transferring from one container to another.

Report the following data:

Weight of Wood Samples   Sample 1:   Sample 2:

Absorbance of Standards and Unknown Samples

COPPER (324.7 nm)   ARSENIC (193.7 nm)

0 μg/mL
5 μg/mL
10 μg/mL
15 μg/mL
20 μg/mL
25 μg/mL
SAMPLE 1
SAMPLE 2

Prepare a standard curve for both copper and arsenic and fasten the graph paper to this report sheet.

For each of the two samples extracted, find the copper absorbance on the copper standard curve and the arsenic absorbance on the arsenic standard curve. Record the corresponding concentration on the next page of the report sheet.

Concentration of Metal in Extract Solution

	COPPER	ARSENIC
Sample 1:		
Sample 2:		

Concentration of Metal in Wood

	COPPER	ARSENIC
Sample 1:		
Sample 2:		

Discussion

Identify and **discuss** possible sources of error in this experiment which could lead to incorrect or inaccurate results. Whenever possible, indicate whether the experimental error being described would tend to cause high results, low results, or both high and low lack of precision.

Effect of Heavy Metal Ions on the Growth of Microorganisms

General Discussion

Yeasts are microorganisms which can grow under aerobic or anaerobic conditions. They thrive in the presence of oxygen but will rapidly deplete the oxygen in a closed system. They continue to grow obtaining the energy they need for metabolism from fermentation of carbohydrates.

The fermentation of glucose may be represented by the following equation:

$$C_6H_{12}O_6 \longrightarrow 2C_2H_5OH + 2CO_2 + energy$$

In this experiment we will allow yeast to grow in the presence of glucose. Growth of the microorganism is estimated by measurement of the evolution of carbon dioxide gas. The relative rate of yeast metabolism in several different systems can be estimated by comparing the relative amounts of CO_2 evolved in each system over a given time period.

Heavy metals such as mercury, lead, copper, and arsenic are metabolic poisons in that they inhibit the activity of certain enzymes involved in the metabolic process. In this experiment we will observe the effect that copper and mercury have on yeast metabolism when compared to a metal ion with very low toxicity such as sodium.

Reagents

a. **Metal chlorides.** Sodium chloride, copper(II) chloride, and mercury(II) chloride.

b. **Glucose.**

c. **Yeast.** One packet of dry baker's yeast per student group.

Apparatus (eight per student group)

a. **Plastic or glass syringes.** Monoject® plastic 60-mL syringes are safe and have printing molded into the plastic barrel which minimizes rubbing away of the lettering after repeated usage. Glass syringes having a capacity of 30 mL produce somewhat more consistent volume readings than plastic syringes because the glass plungers slide with less resistance. However, glass syringes are breakable and more costly. Plastic syringe plungers slide best if lubricated with stopcock grease.

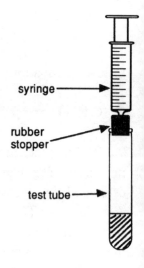

syringe

rubber stopper

test tube

b. **Culture tubes (16×150 mm).**

c. **Rubber stoppers (1-hole) size "0".** Should snugly fit both the culture tube and the syringe Luer tip.

If the syringe has a collar around the Luer tip, the collar should be cut off with a sharp knife or single-edge razor blade. The syringe is connected to the test tube as shown in the diagram. The best approach is to put the stopper snugly into the tube and then the syringe into the stopper.

Procedure

a. **Preparation of sodium, copper, and mercury solutions.** Calculate the weights of sodium chloride, copper(II) chloride, and mercury(II) chloride needed to prepare 100 mL of separate solutions containing 1000 mg of each metal ion per liter. Prepare and label these three solutions using 100-mL volumetric flasks. Smaller volumes such as 10 mL or 25 mL may be prepared to minimize heavy metal usage.

b. **Glucose solution.** Prepare a solution containing 20 g glucose in 100 mL of water warmed to 40 °C. Note: Do not overheat because doing so may kill the yeast organisms.

c. **Culture tube preparation.** Prepare labeled culture tubes as follows:

Tube number

1	1.0 mL of deionized water (Blank)
2	2.0 mL of deionized water (Blank)
3	1.0 mL of sodium chloride solution
4	2.0 mL of sodium chloride solution
5	1.0 mL of copper(II) chloride solution
6	2.0 mL of copper(II) chloride solution
7	1.0 mL of mercury(II) chloride solution
8	2.0 mL of mercury(II) chloride solution

d. **Yeast/glucose mixture.** Add one package of dry baker's yeast (or 20 g of refrigerated cake yeast) to the glucose solution described in part **b**. Stir well with a stirring rod or preferably with a magnetic stirrer for 4-5 minutes. **Note:** Yeast which is nearing or has exceeded its expiration date tends to produce slower carbon dioxide evolution.

e. **Addition of yeast/glucose mixture.** Add 10.0 mL of yeast/glucose mixture to each of the culture tubes, insert the stopper followed by the syringe, and invert to mix. To ensure that yeast is distributed uniformly to all eight tubes, continue stirring until the last 10-mL aliquot has been measured. Stand the tubes in a test tube rack or in flasks. Try to prepare all 8 tubes as quickly as possible immediately after the 4-5 minute stirring of the yeast/glucose mixture. Record the time at which the syringes are connected to the tubes. This corresponds to the initial time (t = 0) at which the syringe volume readings should be 0.0 mL.

As the yeast cells begin metabolizing glucose, changes in the mixtures occur. **Record observations.** At regular intervals (5 minutes is recommended), record the total volume of gas evolved by each solution by reading the syringe plunger position on the syringe barrel. Wear safety glasses because pressure in the tubes could cause the stopper to pop from the tube. Continue recording gas volume and time for a period of 30 to 45 minutes. Record the **data** for each test tube in a systematic fashion in the lab notebook.

Waste Disposal

Copper and mercury solutions should be disposed of in the waste heavy metal container. All other solutions may be rinsed down the drain with water.

Data and Discussion:

Calculate the concentrations of sodium, copper(II), and of mercury(II) ions in those tubes where they were used. Tubes 1 and 2 serve as blanks because none of the three cations were added.

Do the three metal ions affect yeast metabolism to a different degree? Does the rate of carbon dioxide evolution change as the concentration of the metal ion changes? For tubes 2, 4, 6, and 8, prepare plots of volume of gas (in mL) on the y axis versus time in minutes on the x-axis. Draw a best-fit straight line through the data points for each plot, and estimate the rate of CO_2 evolution (mL/min) from the slope of each plot.

Wastewater treatment plants use microorganisms to consume organic compounds in the wastewater. Why is it important that high concentrations of toxic chemicals such as heavy metals and pesticides not be thrown down drains or sewers thereby allowing them to reach municipal wastewater plants?

Analysis of Phosphate in Water

General Discussion

In the present experiment, we will analyze a series of natural water samples for their phosphate content. Detergents are among the greatest contributors to phosphate content in rivers and lakes because phosphate containing compounds are used in detergent formulation as water softeners (builders). Phosphate is not toxic to animals or plants. In fact, it is a plant nutrient which stimulates the growth of aquatic weeds and algae. This may cause lakes and rivers to become clogged and overrun with plants.

The principle of this method involves the formation of molybdophosphoric acid, which is reduced to the intensely colored complex, molybdenum blue. This analytical method is extremely sensitive and is reliable down to concentrations below 0.1 mg phosphorus per liter.

Apparatus

The Spectronic 20 spectrophotometer will be employed in the measurement of color intensity of the blue solutions.

A wavelength of 650 nanometers will be used in these analyses.

Reagents

a. **Ammonium molybdate reagent:** (prepared by instructor) The solution is prepared by dissolving 25 g of $(NH_4)_6Mo_7O_{24} \cdot 4H_2O$ in 175 mL purified water. Cautiously, 280 mL of concentrated H_2SO_4 is added to 400 mL of purified water. The acid solution is cooled, the molybdate solution is added, and the entire mixture is diluted to 1 liter.

b. **Stannous chloride reagent:** (prepared by instructor) 2.5 g of $SnCl_2 \cdot 2H_2O$ is dissolved in 100 mL of glycerine. The mixture is gently heated to hasten dissolution.

c. **Stock 20.0 mg/L phosphate solution:** (prepared by instructor) To prepare this solution, 0.286 g of KH_2PO_4 is dissolved in 1.0 liter of water. This is a 200 mg/L stock solution. Then dilute 100 mL of this solution to 1.0 liter.

Procedure

Note: Glassware should be washed thoroughly with hot water followed by rinsing with purified water. Do not use phosphate-containing detergents to clean equipment for this experiment.

16

Prepare the following standard phosphate solutions:

a. **1.0 mg/L standard:** Place 2.00 mL of 20.0 mg/L phosphate solution in a 100-mL graduated cylinder and dilute to 40 mL with purified water. (Save exactly 25 mL in an erlenmeyer flask for analysis with the spectrophotometer.)

b. **2.0 mg/L standard:** Place 4.00 mL of 20.0 mg/L phosphate solution in a 100-mL graduated cylinder and dilute to 40 mL with purified water. (Save exactly 25 mL in an erlenmeyer flask for analysis with the spectrophotometer.)

c. **3.0 mg/L standard:** Repeat the directions for the 1.0 mg/L standard using 6.00 mL of 20.0 mg/L phosphate. (Save 25 mL)

d. **4.0 mg/L standard:** Repeat the directions for the 1.0 mg/L standard using 8.00 mL of 20.0 mg/L phosphate. (Save 25 mL)

e. **5.0 mg/L standard:** Repeat the directions for the 1.0 mg/L standard using 10.00 mL of 20.0 mg/L phosphate (Save 25 mL).

f. **Blank:** Set aside 25 mL of purified water which will be treated with the color developing reagent to serve as a blank.

These five standard solutions and the blank should now be treated according to the following "color development" procedure. After measuring the absorbance of these solutions, make a plot of absorbance versus concentration as described by your instructor.

Color Development in Sample:

This procedure is used for the *five standard solutions* and for *any river, lake, or sewage water samples* which are to be analyzed for phosphate.

Place in an erlenmeyer flask 25 mL of the water sample to be analyzed. Put 1.00 mL (using a pipet) of ammonium molybdate solution into the flask and swirl to mix. To the flask add 2 drops of stannous chloride solution and mix by swirling. If phosphate is present, a blue color will develop to a maximum in 5 minutes.

Note: The time period is somewhat critical. Measurements should be taken anywhere from 5 to 15 minutes after addition of stannous chloride.

While you are waiting for the blue color to develop, set the wavelength to 650 nm on the spectrophotometer. Use the blank solution to set it to read zero absorbance. Using 650 nanometers wavelength, measure the absorbance (after 5-10 minutes color development) of the blue sample.[*]

---

[*] Should one of your samples produce a very dark blue color which can not be read with the spectrophotometer, dilute the original water sample 100 fold. This is accomplished by placing 1.0 mL of the water sample in a 100-mL graduated cylinder and then adding enough purified water to bring the volume up to 100 mL. Now 25 mL of this diluted sample may be analyzed according to directions for color development in sample, previously given. Remember that the concentration which you ultimately obtain from this sample will have to be multiplied by 100 because of the 100 fold dilution.

Waste Disposal

All solutions may be rinsed down the drain with water.

Calculations

From the concentration and the absorbance of the five standards and the blank, make a plot of absorbance as a function of concentration (a "standard curve" or "Beer's Law plot"). Use the plot and the absorbance of each river, lake, sewage, or unknown solution to determine the concentration in milligrams phosphate ion per liter (mg/L PO_4^{3-} in that sample. We sometimes use concentration units of parts per million (ppm) synonymously with mg/L because 1.0 liter of water at room temperature weighs 1000 grams (to two significant figures). Thus 1.0 mg is one millionth of the weight of one liter. For the sake of consistency in this manual we use units of mg/L and related units such as μg/mL and μg/L.

Report the following data:

Sources of Water Samples

1. _____
2. _____
3. _____
4. _____

Absorbance of Standards:

Blank _____

1.0 mg/L PO_4^{3-} _____

2.0 mg/L PO_4^{3-} _____

3.0 mg/L PO_4^{3-} _____

4.0 mg/L PO_4^{3-} _____

5.0 mg/L PO_4^{3-} _____

Note: Prepare a standard curve and turn it in with the report sheet.

Absorbance of Water Samples   Dilution Factor (if any)

1. _____   _____
2. _____   _____
3. _____   _____
4. _____   _____

Concentration of Phosphate in Water Samples

1. _____   3. _____

2. _____   4. _____

Discussion

Identify those aspects of the procedure which may have introduced some error into the final results. In each case indicate whether the error would cause the measured value to be too high, too low, or either.

Phosphates in Detergents

General Discussion

Excess phosphates are known to accelerate the natural aging of lakes (eutrophication) and also present a serious pollution problem by encouraging excessive growth of aquatic plants. They enter waterways as runoff from agricultural lands as fertilizer and as human and animal waste. The largest source of phosphorous entering the environment is synthetic detergents which contain phosphate compounds to soften water, increase the pH of water, and increase surfactant efficiency. About 7.5 billion pounds of detergents were used in the United States in 1991. This source accounts for over 2 billion pounds of phosphorus which is nearly half the phosphorous entering our waters. Sodium tripolyphosphate (STPP) is most widely used, and ordinary detergents may contain up to 50% of it by weight. Automatic dishwasher detergents require high levels of STPP because it effectively prevents water spotting during the drying process.

As of 1992, 30 states, containing about half the population of the U.S., have either limited or were considering limiting the use of phosphates. The use of phosphates in U.S. and Canadian home laundry detergents continues to decline. However, even with limitations on phosphates in detergents, specialty cleaners, such as automatic dishwasher detergents and institutional products, are still allowed to contain high amounts of phosphorus or phosphate compounds. Consequently, lakes continue to develop green algae blooms in the summer due to high phosphorus levels in the lake water.

This experiment allows us to see how manufacturers have responded to public and congressional pressure and it provides an opportunity to determine if detergent formulas meet standards set by local law. The experimental procedure consists of combustion of a detergent sample and titrating phosphate using a special mixed indicator to determine the endpoint.

Reagents and Apparatus

a. buret
b. hotplate
c. concentrated HCl
d. two crucibles (porcelain or ceramic fiber)
e. mixed indicator solution:
    32 parts 0.05% methyl orange
    32 parts 0.05% phenolphthalein
    8 parts 0.04% thymol blue
    4 parts 0.1% methylene blue
    24 parts ethanol
f. 50% NaOH
g. standardized 0.2 N NaOH
h. muffle furnace (capable of heating to 700 °C)

Procedure

Sample preparation

Place about 2 grams of detergent in a crucible and record the exact weight of detergent on your report sheet. The weight may be determined by subtracting the empty weight of the crucible from the weight of the crucible plus detergent.

Note: Some nonphosphate products contain builders which interfere with this procedure. It is recommended that an automatic dishwasher detergent or institutional product known to contain phosphorus be examined.

Heat the crucible and contents (without lid) until burning and smoke subsides. If possible, this should be done in a hood to expel the foul smelling fumes. Then heat at 700 °C in a muffle furnace for at least 10 minutes. Be sure to wear protective gloves and use tongs when placing your crucible in the furnace and when removing it. After cooling, transfer the contents to a 250-mL erlenmeyer flask and rinse the crucible with three 5 mL portions of concentrated HCl. Add the rinsings to the flask.

Heat the flask on a hotplate almost to dryness. Avoid splashing. After cooling, add 50 mL of purified water and 10 mL of concentrated hydrochloric acid, cover with a watch glass, and boil gently for about 10 minutes. Allow the solution to cool and filter using vacuum filtration, washing the filter paper with several 10-mL aliquots of purified water. After dilution to 100 mL, the solution is ready to be adjusted to the starting pH.

Repeat the above procedure with a second detergent in a second crucible.

Titration

Add 1 mL of indicator to the solution. It will turn light red, indicating that the principal species in solution is H_3PO_4. Add 50% sodium hydroxide to convert H_3PO_4 to $H_2PO_4^-$ and continue addition until a pH of about 4 is reached; the indicator will appear orange. Now add dilute (about 0.2 N) prepared by instructor sodium hydroxide until pH is exactly 4.3. This corresponds to a marked color change from orange to yellow (just before yellow-green). *The instructor will demonstrate the titration at the beginning of the laboratory period and will discuss the indicator color changes to be expected. Indicator paper will also be provided for pH determination during the initial stages of the pH adjustment to pH=4.*

A pH of 4.3 corresponds to the endpoint of the reaction:

$$H_3PO_4 + OH^- \longrightarrow H_2PO_4^- + H_2O$$

This is the starting point of the actual titration. The endpoint of the titration is at pH 8.8:

$$H_2PO_4^- + OH^- \longrightarrow HPO_4^= + H_2O$$

Thus, when the solution is adjusted to pH 4.3, it is ready to be titrated to the endpoint which occurs at a pH of exactly 8.8 or an indicator change from yellow-green to pink. The amount of phosphate corresponds to the amount of base used between the pH 4.3 and 8.8 endpoints. In case of minor overtitrations (where no solutions have been spilled), additional acid can be added and the solution can be adjusted to a pH of 4.3 and retitrated. Initial volume and acid concentration are irrelevant because the titration is carried out between two endpoints.

Waste Disposal

All solutions may be rinsed down the drain with water.

Calculations

Percentages as % STPP, % phosphate, and % phosphorus may be calculated using the general formula

$$\frac{N \times mL \times W}{\text{(weight of sample)}}$$

where N equals the normality of the base, mL the titration value in milliliters between endpoints, and W the milliequivalent weight (equivalent weight/1000): 0.1226 for STPP ($Na_5P_3O_{10}$), 0.0950 for the phosphate ion (PO_4^{3-}), and 0.03097 for phosphorus (P). A sample calculation for percent phosphate in 2.25 grams of detergent is

$$\frac{[(0.200 \text{ meq / mL}) (25.7 \text{ mL}) (0.0950 \text{ g / meq})]}{2.25 \text{ g}} \times 100 = 21.7\%$$

Record the concentration as % STPP, % PO_4^{3-} and % phosphorus for each of your two detergent samples.

As with previous experiments, identify sources of possible error, and indicate whether these errors would tend to cause high results or low results.

Report the following data:

Identity of Detergent Samples

1. _____
2. _____

Exact Weights of Samples	1		2	
crucible + contents		g		g
empty crucible		g		g
weight of detergent		g		g

Titration Results	1		2	
final buret reading		mL		mL
initial buret reading		mL		mL
volume of titrant		mL		mL

Calculated Percentages	1		2	
percent $Na_5P_3O_{10}$		%		%
percent PO_4^{3-}		%		%
percent P		%		%

Discussion

How do your results compare with the phosphorus content of the product as indicated by the manufacturer? What are the main sources of error in this procedure? Indicate whether these errors would tend to cause high results or low results.

Determination of Nitrate Ion in Water

General Discussion

Nitrate nitrogen may be present in small amounts in fresh domestic wastewater. However, it is seldom found in influents to treatment plants because the nitrate serves as an oxygen source in the biologically unstable wastewater. On the other hand, nitrate is often found in the effluents of biological treatment plants, because it represents the final form of nitrogen from the oxidation of organic nitrogen compounds. Trickling-filter and activated sludge treatment plant effluents may contain from 0 to 50 mg/L nitrate, depending on the total nitrogen content of the influent, the degree of loading, and the temperature of the sewage.

Nitrate may also be found in river water, lake water, and most importantly in ground water. The nitrate may originate from sewage, or in rural areas, it may be produced by fertilizer or barnyard runoff. The U.S. Public Health Service designated safe limit for nitrate in water is 45 mg/L nitrate or 10 mg/L nitrate nitrogen. Nitrate in drinking water is particularly dangerous to small children, infants, and fetuses.

In this experiment, nitrate will be reduced to nitrite with zinc. The nitrite reacts with sulfanilic acid and N-1-naphthylethylenediamine to produce a red compound. The intensity of the red color is analyzed spectrophotometrically. The amount of zinc and the contact period are important.

Special Apparatus

a. **Spectronic 20** - spectrophotometer set at 550 nm.

b. **Filter paper and vacuum filtration apparatus.**

Reagents

(All of the following are prepared by the instructor or lab technician and are available for student use in the experiment.)

a. **Stock potassium nitrate solution**: 0.816 g of anhydrous KNO_3 is dissolved in purified water and diluted to 1 liter to produce a 500 mg/L nitrate solution. 100 mL of this solution is diluted to 1 liter to produce the stock **50 mg/L nitrate** solution which will be used in this experiment.

b. **Hydrochloric acid diluted 1:4**: 1 part con. HCl and 4 parts water.

c. **Sulfanilic acid**: Dissolve 0.60 g of sulfanilic acid in 70 mL hot purified water, cool, dilute to 100 mL with purified water, and mix thoroughly.

d. **Zinc**: Add 1.000 g finely powdered zinc to 200 g sodium chloride, NaCl, in a bottle and mix thoroughly by shaking for several minutes.

e. **N-1-naphthylethylenediamine dihydrochloride reagent**: Dissolve 0.60 g N-1-naphthylethylenediamine dihydrochloride in purified water to which 1.0 mL con. HCl has been added. Dilute to 100 mL and mix. Store in refrigerator. (Stable for about a week.)

f. **Sodium acetate solution**: Prepare 100 mL of 2 M $NaC_2H_3O_2$.

Procedure

a. **Preparation of standards**:

Blank: Measure 50 mL of purified water and transfer to a 250-mL erlenmeyer flask.

2.5 mg/L standard: Add 2.5 mL of stock 50 mg/L nitrate solution to a 100-mL graduated cylinder. Add purified water and dilute to a volume of 50 mL. Transfer to a 250-mL erlenmeyer flask.

5.0 mg/L standard: Repeat the directions for the 2.5 mg/L standard using 5.0 mL of 50 mg/L nitrate solution.

10.0 mg/L standard: Repeat the directions for the 2.5 mg/L standard using 10.0 mL of 50 mg/L nitrate solution.

15.0 mg/L standard: Repeat the directions for the 2.5 mg/L standard using 15.0 mL of 50 mg/L nitrate solution.

b. **Experimental**: Use the following procedure for treating standards as well as river, lake, well, or sewage water samples.

Note: Treated sewage effluent may require a 5-fold or a 10-fold dilution. A 10-fold dilution can be performed by pipetting 5.0 mL of the treated wastewater (sewage) sample into a 100-mL graduated cylinder and adding enough water to bring the volume up to 50 mL. This 50 mL sample can then be taken through the experimental and color development procedure. A 10-fold dilution results in a dilution factor of 10. Remember to multiply the concentration obtained for the diluted sample by a factor of 5 or 10.

To a 50.0-mL water sample in a 250-mL erlenmeyer flask, add 1.0 mL of dilute HCl (1:4 dilution) and 1.0 mL sulfanilic acid reagent and mix thoroughly. In a dry 10-mL graduated cylinder, measure one mL of the Zn/NaCl granular mixture and add it to the erlenmeyer flask.

Swirl the flask for seven minutes. Filter with a vacuum flask after the seven minute swirling period. Rinse the erlenmeyer flask well with purified water and pour the filtered water sample back into the flask.

Color Development: Add 1.0 mL N-1-naphthyl-ethylenediamine dihydrochloride reagent to the filtered sample and mix. Add 1.0 mL of 2 M sodium acetate solution and mix. Allow 5 minutes (or more) for color development.

Spectrophotometric Measurement: Measure the color intensity with a spectrophotometer at a wavelength of 550 nm. Purified water may be used for a blank unless the water sample is cloudy. In that case, use a sample of cloudy water as a blank. Record the absorbance of the colored sample.

Waste Disposal

All solutions may be rinsed down the drain with water.

Calculations

From the concentration and the absorbance of the four standards, make a plot of absorbance as a function of concentration. Use the plot and the absorbance of each unknown solution to determine the concentration in mg/L nitrate ion (mg NO_3^-/L) in that sample. Also, express the concentration in terms of mg/L of nitrate nitrogen (mg N/L) in the sample.

Discussion

Identify and discuss possible sources of error in this experiment. How does each kind of error affect the final answer in terms of making it too high, too low or either?

Also, use the concentrations of nitrate nitrogen measured in each water sample to estimate the drinking water quality (from the standpoint of nitrate content) of each of the samples tested.

Report the following data:

Sources of Water Samples

1. _____
2. _____
3. _____
4. _____

Absorbance of Standards

    2.5 mg/L NO_3^- _____

    5.0 mg/L NO_3^- _____

    10.0 mg/L NO_3^- _____

    15.0 mg/L NO_3^- _____

Note: Prepare a standard curve and turn it in with the report sheet.

Absorbance of Water Samples (if any)	Dilution Factor
1. _____	_____
2. _____	_____
3. _____	_____
4. _____	_____

Concentration of Nitrate in Water Samples

	as NO_3^-	as N
1.	_____	_____
2.	_____	_____
3.	_____	_____
4.	_____	_____

Discussion

Identify and discuss sources of error in this experiment. How would you rate the quality of the water samples tested in this experiment?

Ion Selective Electrodes

A. The pH meter

General Discussion

The pH of an aqueous solution may be easily measured with a pH meter by immersing two electrodes, or a combination electrode, into a container of the water sample. The reference electrode supplies a constant potential and the glass electrode (which is sensitive to H^+) supplies a variable potential depending on the H^+ ion concentration. The pH meter is calibrated with standard buffer solutions having known pH values. The pH meter gives a much more precise measurement of pH than indicator paper and is used when an accurate determination is needed.

Apparatus

a. **Sargent model PBL pH meter.**

b. **Combination electrode** for pH measurement.

c. **Carrying case for pH meter** including plastic bottles for buffer, a beaker, and a wash bottle filled with purified water. This material is only necessary if the analyses are to be carried out in the field rather than in the laboratory.

Reagents

a. **Buffer solution**, pH = 4.01: Prepare a 0.05 M potassium hydrogen phthalate ($KHC_8O_4H_4$) solution by dissolving 2.551 g of the salt in sufficient water to make a volume of 250 mL. (Use a volumetric flask.)

b. **Sodium hydroxide**, 0.10 M: Dissolve 4.00 g of solid sodium hydroxide in enough water to prepare a liter of solution. (Use a 1.00 liter volumetric flask.)

c. **Potassium dihydrogen phosphate**, 0.10 M: Dissolve 3.402 g of KH_2PO_4 in enough water to prepare 250 mL of solution. (Use a 250-mL volumetric flask.)

d. **Buffer solution**, pH = 7.00: Add 29.0 mL of 0.10 M NaOH to 50.0 mL of 0.10 M KH_2PO_4. This is easily accomplished by pouring 0.10 M KH_2PO_4 into a graduated cylinder until the liquid reaches the 50-mL mark. Then 0.10 M NaOH is added to the graduate until the total volume of the mixture is 79 mL.

Procedure

Use the following steps to analyze water samples and commercial products. The samples to be tested may include river water, treated sewage, waste water plant influent and effluent, vinegar, lemon juice, Coca-Cola™, household ammonia, baking soda, Tide™, etc. (For solid materials, dissolve a spatula-full in 5 mL purified water.)

a. Set up the instrument for either line or battery operation by sliding the power switch in back of the meter to either A.C. or BATT.

b. Turn the Operation Switch to pH.

c. Immerse the electrodes in pH = 7.0 buffer.

d. Set the Temperature Dial to the temperature of the buffer.

e. Use the Calibration Control to set the meter reading to exactly 7.00.

f. Rinse the electrode.

g. Immerse the electrodes in the pH = 4.01 buffer.

h. The meter should read 4.01. If it does not, use a screwdriver to adjust the slope control to give a reading of 4.01.

i. Set the Temperature Control to the temperature of the water sample to be analyzed. Place the electrodes in the sample. Read the pH of the sample directly.

WARNING - Handle the combination electrodes very cautiously. They are **VERY FRAGILE** and cost about $50.00.

B. Determination of Fluoride Ion in Water Using the Fluoride Ion Selective Electrode

General Discussion

Fluoride ion has been shown to aid in the development of cavity resistant teeth. Consequently, many communities are now adding about 1 mg/L of fluoride (in the form of NaF) to their water supplies. However, too much fluoride can lead to deformed and/or discolored teeth. It is essential that the fluoride ion concentration not exceed 1 mg/L to prevent these unwanted side effects.

The fluoride electrode is a rapid sensing, sensitive, and accurate tool for measuring fluoride in water. We will use it to test municipal water and other samples to determine whether fluoride concentrations are at the proper level.

Apparatus

a. **pH meter with expanded scale capability.**

b. **Fluoride combination electrode.**

c. **Magnetic stirring bar and stirring motor.**

Reagents

a. **100 mg/L F⁻ solution**: Weigh out exactly 0.221 g of sodium fluoride (NaF) and dilute to 1.00 L in a volumetric flask.

Fluoride Procedure

a. Preparation of Standards

1.0 mg/L F⁻ standard: Add with a pipet 1.00 mL of 100 mg/L F⁻ solution to a 100-mL graduated cylinder. Add purified water and dilute to a volume of 100.0 mL.

5.0 mg/L F⁻ standard: Repeat the directions for the 1.0 mg/L standard using 5.0 mL of 100 mg/L F solution.

b. Experimental

Obtain about 50 mL of each water sample to be tested for fluoride. These samples will be analyzed immediately after calibrating the meter.

Calibration: The fluoride ion electrode should be connected to a specific ion meter. Use the 2 point calibration procedure as outlined by the instructor to calibrate the instrument with the two standards.

Sample Measurements: Rinse and blot the electrode, and place it into the first 50 mL unknown water sample. Place the electrode in the solution and read the F⁻ concentration directly in mg/L.

C. Determination of Dissolved Oxygen in Water Using the Oxygen Electrode

General Discussion

The Orion oxygen electrode simplifies the routine measurement of dissolved oxygen by allowing oxygen concentration to be read directly in milligrams per liter on any pH meter. A meter reading of 5.0 is, therefore, equivalent to a DO of 5.0 milligrams per liter. Electrode standardization is carried out in water-saturated air (rather than air-saturated water required for most DO instruments). An electrode zero position allows the electrode to be standardized. The electrode consists of an oxygen sensor, a thermocompensator, battery operated circuits, and operating controls right on the electrode. The electronics of the electrode uses extremely low-drain circuitry so that battery life approaches the battery shelf life. An overflow funnel with a small, attached magnetic stirring bar is also provided with the electrode.

Apparatus

a. **pH meter** - Scale expansion is not required.

b. **Magnetic stirrer.**

c. **BOD sample bottles**, 300 mL (nominal) capacity.

d. **Orion oxygen sensing electrode.**

Procedure

a. Calibration

1. Connect the electrode to the meter.

2. With the electrode mode switch in the OFF position, switch the meter to the pH mode.

3. Set the temperature control to 25 °C.

4. Set the reading to 7.00 with the meter's calibration (standardization) control.

5. Turn the mode switch to BT CK (battery check). Good battery operation is indicated by a reading of 13.0 or greater.

6. Turn the mode switch to "zero" and use the calibration control to set the meter to 0.0.

7. Insert the funnel into a BOD sample bottle containing enough water to just cover the bottom. (This bottle is also used for storage between measurements.) Insert the electrode, making sure that the electrode tip is not immersed in the water and does not have water droplets clinging to the outside of the membrane.

8. Turn the electrode mode switch to the AIR position. Set the meter to 7.60 (760 mm Hg/100).

9. Store the electrode in the air calibration bottle when not in use.

b. Sample Analysis

1. Insert the funnel into a <u>completely filled</u> sample BOD bottle, making sure the funnel is snugly seated. <u>Slowly</u> immerse the standardized electrode into the funnel. Sample displaced by the electrode will collect in the funnel.

2. Place the bottle on a magnetic stirrer and stir gently.

3. Turn the electrode mode switch to H_2O and set the meter to the pH mode.

4. Wait until a stable reading is obtained. Record this value as mg/L dissolved oxygen.

5. Slowly remove the electrode from the funnel. Remove the funnel. Rinse the electrode and funnel with purified water. Gently blot the membrane dry.

Waste Disposal

All solutions may be rinsed down the drain with water.

Report the following data:

A. The pH Meter

<u>Sample</u>   <u>pH</u>

_____   _____

_____   _____

_____   _____

_____   _____

_____   _____

_____   _____

_____   _____

_____   _____

_____   _____

B. Determination of Fluoride in Water Using the Fluoride Ion Selective Electrode

<u>Water Sample</u>   <u>Fluoride Concentration</u>

_____   _____

_____   _____

_____   _____

Unknown 1
Unknown 2

C. Determination of DO in Water Using the Oxygen Electrode

<u>Water Sample</u>   <u>O_2 Concentration</u>

_____   _____

_____   _____

_____   _____

_____   _____

Note: Remember to include correct concentration units whenever appropriate.

Salts (Ionic Compounds) In Water

A. Conductance Of Water And Wastewater

General Discussion

Conductance yields a measure of a water's capacity to convey an electric current. An aqueous system containing ions will conduct an electric current. In a direct-current field the positive ions migrate toward the negative electrode while the negative ions migrate toward the positive electrode. Most inorganic acids, bases, and salts are good conductors. Molecules of organic compounds such as sucrose and ethanol do not dissociate into ions in aqueous solution and therefore produce aqueous solutions which are poor conductors.

Freshly purified water has a conductance of 0.5 to 2 micromhos, rising to a value of 2 to 4 micromhos after a few weeks of storage. The increase results principally from the absorption of atmospheric carbon dioxide and to a lesser extent ammonia.

Most high quality waters have conductances between 50 and 500 μmhos, with highly mineralized water being in the range of 500 to 1000 μmhos and even higher. The relative conductivities of various water samples should be comparable to the total solids determined for the water in Part B of this experiment.

The standard unit of electrical resistance is the ohm. The standard unit of electrical conductance is its inverse, the mho. As expected, 1000 μmhos = 1 mmho. A conductance cell and a Wheatstone bridge are essential for measuring the electrical resistances of the samples.

Instructions Pertaining to Water Samples

For parts A, B, and C of this experiment, the student is expected to analyze 4 - 6 four water samples. In general these samples will be as follows:

a. Water from a nearby river (obtained each week by the instructor or a designated student)

b. Treated water from the Wastewater Treatment Plant (obtained each week by the instructor)

c. One or more unknowns prepared by the instructor

d. A water sample, of the students's own choosing, taken prior to coming to lab

Each sample should be identified in a conspicuous place in the student's report sheet.

Apparatus

a. **Conductivity Meter**

b. **Conductivity Cell:** Platinum electrode type

Procedure

For each sample to be studied, prepare two regular test tubes each filled to about one inch from the top with the sample. Rinse the conductance cell in one test tube of the first water sample being sure that the rinsing is very thorough. Measure the conductivity of the second test tube full of the first sample. Proceed in the same way until all the water samples have been measured. Record the conductance in micromhos on the report sheet.

Use Table 3 (next page) to estimate the concentration of sodium chloride in milligrams per liter that is equivalent to each observed conductivity. You may have to interpolate.

B. Total Solids

General Discussion

Although some water contaminants may be gases (like dissolved ammonia) or liquids (like oil), the majority of the common contaminants are dissolved or suspended solids. Sea water (although it may not necessarily be polluted) has an overall dissolved salt content of 35,000 mg/L. In general, water is considered to be a salt water if it contains over 3,000 mg/L dissolved solids, brackish water it it contains 500-3,000 mg/L dissolved solids, and fresh water if it contains less than 500 mg/L.

Table 3: Selected Parameters of Water Quality			
Specific conductance Micromhos/cm*	Specific resistance megohm-cm*	Milligrams per Liter NaCl†	Grains of Calcium Carbonate per gallon
.055	18.240	none	none
.056	18.000	.022	.002
.063	16.000	.025	.002
.071	14.000	.029	.002
.083	12.000	.033	.002
.100	10.000	.040	.003
.125	8.000	.050	.004
.167	6.000	.067	.005
.250	4.000	.100	.007
.500	2.000	.200	.015
1.000	1.000	.400	.029
1.250	.800	.500	.037
1.667	.600	.667	.049
2.500	.400	1.000	.073
5.000	.200	2.000	.146
10.000	.100	4.000	.292
20.000	.050	8.000	.585
40.000	.025	16.000	1.170
80.000	.0125	32.000	2.340
158.730	.0063	63.492	4.641
312.500	.0032	125.000	9.137
625.000	.0016	250.000	18.273
1,250.000	.0008	500.000	36.550
2,500.000	.0004	1,000.000	73.099
5,000.000	.0002	2,000.000	146.199
10,000.000	.0001	4,000.000	292.398

* At 25 °C
† At 25 °C, given specific conductance values included in this table

In the present experiment, no attempt will be made to determine the nature of any individual dissolved or suspended solid in a water sample. The purpose is simply to measure the combined or total concentration of all solids in milligrams per liter. This experiment will give the student an opportunity to compare the total solids in various types or water - from drinking water to treated waste water. It is also expected that the student will gain some skill in laboratory techniques (like proper use of the analytical balance).

Apparatus

a. **Hot plates**

b. **150-mL beakers**

c. **Analytical balances**

Procedure

Swirl each bottle of water and then obtain a sample which is exactly 50 mL. Swirling is especially important if the water is turbid and appears to contain some suspended solids.

Heat each of four empty beakers on a hot plate and and allow to cool **to room temperature** before measuring the weight of each with an analytical balance. This is to evaporate any volatile materials which may adhere to the glass surface. After recording the weights (to the nearest 0.0001 g) of the empty beakers, pour 50 mL of the first water sample to be analyzed into the first beaker. Do the same with the other beakers and the other water samples. Use the hot plate to gently boil these samples.

After evaporation is complete, use your tongs to place the dry beakers with its contents on a ceramic surface or in a desiccator for cooling. Reduce the heat applied to the beakers just before the point of total dryness is reached. Otherwise, the rapid temperature change could crack a beaker. Care must also be taken to allow all traces of water to evaporate because even one droplet of liquid water will drastically alter the apparent weight of residue in the beaker. When cool, weigh and record the weights of the beakers with residue.

The difference between the weight of a beaker before and after evaporation corresponds to the weight of total solids in the 50-mL water sample. Use the following formula to determine the mg/L of total solids for each sample. Record these values and any calculations.

$$mg/L \text{ total solids} = \frac{\text{grams of total solids}}{\text{mL of sample}} \times 1,000,000$$

Dilute hydrochloric acid may be used to dissolve any residue remaining in the beakers which proves difficult to wash with soap and water.

C. Hardness Of Water And Wastewater

Water containing soluble dipositive ions (Fe^{++}, Mg^{++}, and primarily Ca^{++}) is known as hard water. In addition to adding taste to water, iron in the form of soluble iron (II) is readily oxidized to iron (III) which forms insoluble Fe^{3+}

compounds. It soon forms ugly, hard to remove rust brown stains on plumbing fixtures and clothes. Calcium in hard water is responsible for scale in boilers. Upon heating, calcium is precipitated as calcium carbonate on the boiler sides and in the boiler tubes. The scale is a poor conductor of heat and causes a waste of fuel. Excessive scale deposits may result in boiler explosions. In the case of hot water heaters, excessive boiler scale may cause heater failure due to burning out of the heating element.

General Discussion

For many years, the standard procedure for determining water hardness was the soap hardness test. In this procedure, a standard soap solution was added dropwise to a measured quantity of water and then the mixture shaken. The number of drops of soap solution required to produce a significant foaming was used to calculate the water hardness.

Today hardness producing ions are titrated with the sequestering agent, ethylenediaminetetraacetic acid (EDTA). The accuracy obtainable with this procedure is much more satisfactory than that of the soap hardness test.

Apparatus

a. **Standard EDTA solution (1 mL is equivalent to 10 μg CaCO$_3$/mL for a 100-mL water sample):** Dilute 3.723 g Na$_2$EDTA to 1000 mL in a 1-liter volumetric flask.

b. **Buffer solution:** Dilute 1.179 g Na_2EDTA, 0.780 g $MgSO_4 \cdot H_2O$, 16.9 g NH_4Cl, and 143 mL concentrated NH_4OH to 250 mL.

c. **Eriochrome black T (EBT) indicator.** Mix 1.0 g of the dye [sodium salt of 1-(1-hydroxy-2-naphthylazo)-5-nitro-2-naphthol-4-sulfonic acid] with 100 g of either triethanolamine or 2-methoxyethanol.

d. **Standard Ca solution ($CaCO_3$ 1000 µg/1 mL):** Dissolve 1.000 g $CaCO_3$ in 10 mL 6 M HCl, and dilute to 1.00 liter in a volumetric flask.

e. **50-mL or 25-mL Buret.**

f. **Magnetic stirrer and stirring bar (if available).**

Procedure for Testing Water Hardness by Titration

Rinse a 50-mL buret with about 10 mL of EDTA solution. Mount it in a buret clamp on a ring stand, and fill it to above the 0.0 mark with EDTA solution. Open the valve and carefully withdraw solution into a waste beaker until the bottom of the meniscus stands at exactly 0.0 mL. No bubble should remain in the buret tip. With a 200-mL graduated cylinder measure as accurately as possible 100 mL of the water sample to be tested and pour it into a 250-mL beaker. Add 2 mL of the buffer solution (using a syringe or a 20-mL graduated cylinder) and 10 drops of EBT indicator to the beaker.

Allow EDTA solution to run into the beaker from the buret with stirring until the wine red color of the indicator turns blue. Do not add more than 1 drop excess of EDTA. If the endpoint is overrun, the results will be meaningless, and the titration should be repeated. The volume of EDTA solution is read to the nearest 0.1 mL and recorded on the report sheet. For each 1.0 mL of EDTA solution required, the water contains 10 mg/L of hardness as $CaCO_3$.

Use this titration method to determine the hardness of the four unknown water samples analyzed in parts A and B of this experiment and a known. A "known" solution, containing 250 mg $CaCO_3$/mL, may be prepared by diluting 25.0 mL of the 1000 mg $CaCO_3$ /mL standard solution to 100.0 mL. This solution is analyzed by titrating the 100-mL quantity with EDTA as with the other water samples.

Waste Disposal

All solutions may be rinsed down the drain with water.

A. Report for **Conductance Of Water And Wastewater**

Water Sample Sources

Conductance   **Concentration of NaCl (in mg/L):**
                              See Table 3

1. _____   _____
2. _____   _____
3. _____   _____
4. _____   _____
5. _____   _____
6. _____   _____

B. Report for **Total Solids**

Water Sample Sources

Beaker Weights

	1	2	3	4	5	6
After						
Before						
Diff						

mg/L of Total Solids

Calculations

C. Report for **Hardness Of Water And Wastewater**

Water Sample Sources

Water Hardness

1. Volume of EDTA   _____ mL
   Hardness: _____ mg/L $CaCO_3$
2. Volume of EDTA   _____ mL
   Hardness: _____ mg/L $CaCO_3$
3. Volume of EDTA   _____ mL
   Hardness: _____ mg/L $CaCO_3$
4. Volume of EDTA   _____ mL
   Hardness: _____ mg/L $CaCO_3$
5. Volume of EDTA   _____ mL
   Hardness: _____ mg/L $CaCO_3$
6. Volume of EDTA   _____ mL
   Hardness: _____ mg/L $CaCO_3$

Acidity and Alkalinity of Drinking Water

(Standard Methods for the Examination of Water and Wastewater,
APHA, AWWA, WPCF, 16th edition, p265)

A. Acidity

General Discussion

While pH is a measure of a water sample's deviation from a neutral value of 7.00, it provides little information about a water sample's ability to neutralize acids or bases. The standard procedures for "acidity" and "alkalinity", which have been modified here to fit the time and equipment requirements of a student laboratory, quantitatively provide that information.

The acidity of a water sample is its capacity to neutralize hydroxide ions. Acidity may be caused by mineral acids such as sulfuric acid or hydrochloric acid or by dissolved carbon dioxide. Most commonly in drinking water, carbon dioxide is the principal cause of acidity. Acidity increases the corrosive behavior of water. Drinking water with a high acidity is likely to be corrosive to copper water pipes and to the solder which joins those pipes. High levels of copper and lead in drinking water often occur when acidic water stands in pipes for extended periods of time (such as over night). In addition to creating a possible health hazard due to dissolved metal ions, acidity in water can cause copper plumbing to develop pin hole leaks after a few years.

Acidity is generally measured by titration with sodium hydroxide to an accepted pH value. Phenolphthalein is an acid-base indicator which changes from colorless to a pink (magenta) at a pH of about 8.3. Generally, acidity is measured by titration of a water sample to pH 8.3 with NaOH titrant. Metacresol purple also changes color at pH 8.3, but gives a sharper color change than phenolphthalein. If available, its use is recommended over phenolphthalein. If a water sample is at the alkaline color of the indicator before any titrant is added, then the acidity is zero and the alkalinity of the water should be tested.

Because CO_2 is the most likely cause of acidity in water, the water sample should be collected within a few hours of the time of analysis. The container used to collect the water should be filled completely and closed with an air-tight seal. A clean plastic soft drink bottle with screw cap is suitable for water samples tested in this procedure.

Apparatus

a. **pH meter and calibration standards.**

b. **Magnetic stirrer and stirring bar.**

c. **Volumetric flask:** 1000-mL and 100-mL.

d. Buret: 50-mL, glass.

e. Polyethylene bottle: 1-L.

Reagents

a. Carbon dioxide-free water: For all stock and standard solutions and for dilutions and titrations, water which is free of CO_2 should be used. Boil purified or deionized water for 15 minutes. Allow to cool to room temperature while allowing nitrogen (if available) to slowly bubble through the water as it cools. The stream of nitrogen serves to displace air from the container and prevent carbon dioxide from re-entering the water.

b. Potassium hydrogen phthalate (KHP), 0.05 N: Primary standard grade KHP should be dried for 2 hours at 110 - 120 °C and allowed to cool in a desiccator. Weigh, in a small beaker, about 1.0 g to the nearest 0.1 milligram and transfer quantitatively to a 100-mL volumetric flask by rinsing with CO_2-free water through a funnel into the flask. Dilute to the mark with CO_2-free water. The equivalent weight of KHP is 204.23. Calculate the exact normality of the KHP solution based on the weight diluted in the flask.

c. Standard sodium hydroxide titrant, 0.025 N: For most drinking water samples, relatively dilute NaOH is required. Prepare the solution by weighing 1.0 g of solid NaOH and diluting to 1 liter with CO_2-free water. Standardize against the KHP solution by pipetting 20.00 mL of KHP into an erlenmeyer flask, adding 20 mL CO_2-free water, and titrating with NaOH to a phenolphthalein (colorless to pink) or metacresol purple endpoint. Determine the normality of the NaOH using the equation:

$$(mL \text{ NaOH}) \times (N \text{ NaOH}) = (mL \text{ KHP}) \times (N \text{ KHP})$$

d. **Phenolphthalein indicator solution, 0.5%:** Dissolve 0.5 g of phenolphthalein in 50 mL ethanol and add 50 mL purified or deionized water.

e. **Metacresol purple indicator solution, 0.1%:** Dissolve 0.100 g of metacresol purple in 100 mL water.

Procedure

Begin by obtaining one or more water samples as suggested or provided by the instructor. Measure and record the pH of the water with a calibrated pH meter.

Following cleaning of a 50-mL buret, rinse it with purified water followed by several rinses with 0.025 N NaOH. Fill the buret with the NaOH solution, make sure there are no air bubbles in the tip, and make sure the meniscus is readable at close to 0.00 mL on the buret scale. Measure 100.0 mL of the water sample to be analyzed into a 250-mL erlenmeyer flask with as little splashing or turbulence as possible. A pipet is preferred but a graduated cylinder may be used if no large-volume pipet is available.

Titrate to a phenolphthalein or metacresol-purple endpoint. If the water is highly acidic, smaller volumes of the sample may be titrated as seems appropriate. Do at least duplicate (preferably triplicate) titrations on each sample being investigated. If the alkaline color of the indicator is observed before any titrant is added, report zero acidity and go on to measurement of alkalinity.

Calculation

Acidity is expressed in terms of milligrams of calcium carbonate per liter. These are the same units that are used to express alkalinity and water hardness. For the procedure described here, acidity would be reported as: "The acidity to pH 8.3 = ___ mg $CaCO_3/L$". **Rinse burets with water before storing them.**

$$\text{Acidity} = \frac{(\text{mL NaOH titrant}) \times (\text{normality NaOH}) \times (50,000)}{(\text{mL water sample})}$$

Calculate the mean value for each sample investigated.

B. Alkalinity

General Discussion

Alkalinity is the measure of a water sample's ability to neutralize hydrogen ions (its acid-neutralizing ability). Alkalinity may be caused by dissolved strong bases such as sodium hydroxide or potassium hydroxide (and other hydroxide-containing compounds), and it may also be caused by dissolved carbonates, bicarbonates, borates, and phosphates. The measured alkalinity is the total of all of these species found in a water sample. For the sake of simplicity, it is expressed in terms of mg $CaCO_3/L$

although many species other than dissolved calcium carbonate may actually contribute to the alkalinity.

One important environmental consequence of alkalinity is the ability of a body of water to withstand acidification due to acidic precipitation or atmospheric deposition. A body of water may have a fairly neutral pH, but if its alkalinity is low, it will be readily acidified. A body of water with the same pH but with higher alkalinity will have a greater buffer capacity and, consequently, a greater resistance to acidification.

Apparatus

a. **Magnetic stirrer and stirring bar.**

b. **Volumetric flask:** 1000-mL and 100-mL.

c. **Buret:** 50-mL, glass.

Reagents

a. **Sodium carbonate solution (Na_2CO_3), 0.05 N:** Primary standard grade Na_2CO_3 should be dried for 4 hours at 250 °C and allowed to cool in a desiccator. Weigh, in a small beaker, about 0.25 g to the nearest 0.1 milligram and transfer quantitatively to a 100-mL volumetric flask by rinsing with purified or deionized water through a funnel into the flask. Dilute to the mark with purified or deionized water. The equivalent weight of Na_2CO_3 is 53.00. Calculate the exact normality of the Na_2CO_3 solution based on the weight diluted in the flask.

b. Standard hydrochloric acid titrant, 0.02 N: Transfer 8.3 mL of concentrated (12 N) reagent-grade HCl to a 1000-mL volumetric flask and dilute to the mark with purified or deionized water. This solution has a concentration of about 0.1 N. Dilute 200 mL of 0.1 N HCl to 1000 mL to prepare a solution which is about 0.02 N.

Standardize by pipetting 10.00 mL of 0.05 N Na_2CO_3 solution into a 250-mL erlenmeyer flask and diluting to about 40 mL with purified or deionized water. Bromcresol green changes in color from blue to yellow as it is acidified. The endpoint is intermediate between blue and yellow and appears as a distinct green color. Titrate using bromcresol green as an indicator until a color change from blue to green appears. Determine the normality of the HCl using the equation: (mL HCl) × (N HCl) = (mL Na_2CO_3) × (N Na_2CO_3)

c. Bromcresol green indicator solution, 0.1%: Dissolve 0.100 g of the sodium salt of bromcresol green in 100 mL water.

Procedure

Rinse the 50-mL buret with several rinses with 0.02 N HCl. Fill the buret with the HCl solution, make sure there are no air bubbles in the tip, and make sure the meniscus is readable at close to 0.00 mL on the buret scale. Measure 100.0 mL of the water sample to be analyzed into a 250-mL erlenmeyer flask.

Titrate to a bromcresol green (pH = 4.5) endpoint. If the water is high in alkalinity, smaller volumes of the sample may be titrated as seems appropriate. Do at least duplicate (preferably triplicate) titrations on each sample being investigated. **Rinse burets with water before storing them.**

Calculation

Alkalinity is expressed in terms of milligrams of calcium carbonate per liter.

$$\text{Alkalinity} = \frac{(\text{mL HCL titrant}) \times (\text{normality HCL}) \times (50,000)}{(\text{mL water sample})}$$

Calculate the mean value for each sample investigated.

Waste Disposal

All solutions may be rinsed down the drain with water.

A. Report for **Acidity of Water**

If the normality of the NaOH was student-determined, record all data and calculations.

Record water sample sources and pH of each sample.

Water Acidity (Be sure to show calculations in notebook)

1. Volume of NaOH _____ mL
   Acidity: _____ mg CaCO$_3$/L
2. Volume of NaOH _____ mL
   Acidity: _____ mg CaCO$_3$/L
3. Volume of NaOH _____ mL
   Acidity: _____ mg CaCO$_3$/L

B. Report for **Alkalinity of Water**

If the normality of the HCl was student-determined, record all data and calculations.

Record water sample sources and pH of each sample.

Water Alkalinity (Show calculations)

1. Volume of HCl _____ mL
   Alkalinity: _____ mg CaCO$_3$/L
2. Volume of HCl _____ mL
   Alkalinity: _____ mg CaCO$_3$/L
3. Volume of Hcl _____ mL
   Alkalinity: _____ mg CaCO$_3$/L

Does the pH of the water samples tested allow a prediction of the acidity or alkalinity of the water? Why or why not? What do the results of this experiment allow you to conclude about the water samples tested (compare them)?

Total Coliform Determination by Membrane Filtration

General Discussion

Measurement of the number of coliform bacteria per 100 mL is often used as a criterion in determining the degree of pollution and the sanitary quality of a sample of water. Up to 10,000 organisms per 100 mL is considered permissible by the USPHS, but the desirable level is less than 100 organisms per 100 mL for surface water. Coliform organisms must be virtually absent in drinking water.

The membrane filtration technique is a rapid, reliable method for the detection of coliforms in water. The filter discs are 150 microns thick, have pores of 0.45 micron diameter and have 80% area perforation. The precision of manufacture is such that bacteria larger than 0.47 micron can not pass through. Eighty percent area perforation facilitates rapid filtration.

To test a sample of water, it is passed through one of these filters. All bacteria present in the sample will be retained directly on the filter's surface. The membrane filter is then placed on an absorbent pad saturated with liquid nutrient medium and incubated for 24 ± 2 hours. The organisms on the filter will form colonies which can be counted under a microscope. If a differential medium such as M-HD Endo Agar is used, coliforms will exhibit a characteristic golden metallic sheen.

Materials

a. **Membrane filter assembly (sterile)**

b. **Side arm flask**, 1000-mL, and rubber hose

c. **Sterile plastic Petri dishes**, 50 mm diameter (6 per student)

d. **Sterile pipets** 1-mL and 10-mL

e. **Sterile water**

f. **M-HD Endo Agar** (50 mL) prepared by student groups: Dissolve 2.6 g of Agar powder in 50 mL purified water containing 1.0 mL ethanol. Heat (cautiously) to boiling to dissolve completely. Dispense (while hot) to the lower half of 60 mm Petri dishes. Allow to solidify.

g. **Water samples** - river or lake, treated sewage, untreated sewage

h. **Binocular microscope or magnifying lens**

Procedure

a. Prepare a small plastic Petri dish as follows:

    i. Using a 10-mL pipet aseptically transfer 4.0 mL of M-HD Endo Agar to the bottom of a Petri dish.

b. Assemble a membrane filtering unit as follows:

    i. Aseptically inset the filter holder base into the neck of a one liter sidearm flask.

    ii. With a flamed forceps place a sterile membrane filter disc, grid side up, on the filter holder base.

    iii. Place the filter funnel on top of the membrane filter disc, and secure it to the base with the clamp.

c. Attach the rubber hose to the vacuum outlet and pour approximately 50 mL of sterile water into the funnel by adding about half the contents of a 100-mL graduated cylinder.

d. Pipette 0.1 mL of the water sample to be analyzed into the sterile water in the funnel and filter by applying a vacuum. (A 10^2 or 10^4 dilution may be necessary for sewage samples. This will be advised by the instructor.)

e. Rinse the inner sides of the funnel with approximately 50 mL of sterile water using the last half of the 100 mL which was used in part c.

f. Turn off the vacuum, remove the funnel top, and transfer the filter disc with sterile forceps to the Petri dish of M-HD Endo Agar. <u>Keep the grid side up</u>.

g. Repeat steps a-f using a new Petri dish and a new filter.

h. Repeat steps a-g using 1.0 mL of the water sample to be analyzed.

i. Repeat steps a-g using 10.0 mL of the water sample to be analyzed.

j. Incubate all six Petri dishes at 35°C for 24 ± 2 hours. Keep them upside down.

k. After incubation, remove the Petri dish cover and place the dish containing the filter on the platform of a binocular microscope.

l. Count the colonies on the discs containing 20-200 colonies with low power magnification, using reflected light. The typical coliform colony has a metallic surface sheen. Ignore any colonies which lack this sheen. If there are more than 200 colonies on a filter, the report should be TNTC (too numerous to count).

Waste Disposal

All solutions may be rinsed down the drain with water. Gelled agar and petri dishes with coliform colonies should be discarded in waste baskets.

Calculations

The calculated coliform density is reported in terms of coliforms per 100 mL. The computation is based upon the membrane filter count within the 20-200 coliform colony range and is made by use of the following equation:

$$\text{Total coliforms} / 100 \text{ ml} = \frac{\text{coliform colonies counted} \times 100}{\text{mL sample filtered}}$$

Report the following data:

Identity of water samples analyzed

	Run #1	Run #2
mL water used	# colonies counted	# colonies counted
0.1 mL	_____	_____
1.0 mL	_____	_____
10.0 mL	_____	_____
100.0 mL (if done)	_____	_____
dilution factor (if any)	_____	_____

Calculated Coliform Density

Run #1 _____
Run #2 _____

Average Coliform density _____

Error Analysis

How may error be introduced into this experiment? Identify important sources of error, and indicate how they may influence the final outcome of the experiment.

Measurement of Dissolved Oxygen, BOD, and Rate of Oxygen Absorption in Water

(a modification of McCormic, *J. Chem. Educ.*, **49** 1972, 839-841)

General Discussion

The solubility of oxygen in water is quite low under ordinary atmospheric pressure and temperature conditions. Oxygen makes up 21% of the volume of the atmosphere which means that its partial pressure is 0.21 atmosphere when atmospheric pressure is one atmosphere. At 20°C and an oxygen partial pressure of 0.21 atm, the solubility of oxygen in water is only 0.0092 g/L (9.2 mg/L). Like all gases, oxygen's solubility decreases as the temperature of water increases. This can be seen in the following table.

Temperature (°C)	Concentration of Dissolved Oxygen (mg O_2/L)
0	14.6
10	11.3
20	9.2
30	6.1

Oxygen concentration in water can be measured by means of an oxygen-sensing electrode, spectrophoto-metrically, and titrimetrically. This experiment uses a titration technique which was first published by Winkler. The method involves several oxidation-reduction reactions, the first of which involves the oxidation of manganese(II) ion by dissolved oxygen to form manganese(III) hydroxide.

$$4Mn^{2+} + O_2 + 8OH^- + 2H_2O \longrightarrow 4Mn(OH)_3 \qquad (I)$$

In the presence of sulfuric acid, manganese(III) ion oxidizes iodide to iodine followed by the reaction of iodine with iodide to form the yellow-brown triiodide ion.

$$2Mn(OH)_3 + 3H_2SO_4 + 2I^- \longrightarrow 2Mn^{2+} + 3SO_4^{2-} + I_2 + 6H_2O \quad (II)$$

$$I_2 + I^- \longrightarrow I_3^- \qquad (III)$$

The iodine (in the form of triiodide) is then titrated with thiosulfate forming iodide and tetrathionate.

$$I_3^- + 2S_2O_3^{2-} \longrightarrow 3I^- + S_4O_6^{2-} \qquad (IV)$$

Adding all of the above equations leads to the following overall reaction stoichiometry:

$$O_2 + 4S_2O_3^{2-} + 2H_2SO_4 \longrightarrow 2S_4O_6^{2-} + 2SO_4^{2-} + 2H_2O \quad (V)$$

It is apparent that 4 thiosulfate ions are required for every O_2 molecule. Each mole of thiosulfate used represents 8 grams (0.25 mole) of oxygen. Thus, the following equation holds true:

$$\text{g } O_2/\text{mole } S_2O_3^{2-})(\text{liters } S_2O_3^{2-})(\text{moles } S_2O_3^{2-}/\text{liter}) = \text{g } O_2 \quad \text{(VI)}$$

This Experiment allows for the measurement of dissolved oxygen in one or more water samples and it provides the option of measuring the (1) the BOD of a wastewater sample and/or (2) the rate of absorption of oxygen by a water sample which has been depleted of oxygen.

Materials

a. **Manganese(II) solution (0.22 M).** Prepare by dissolving the appropriate amount of manganous chloride or manganous sulfate in purified water.

b. **Basic iodide solution (0.3 M) containing sodium azide.** Dissolve 45 g NaI (or 50 g of KI), 24 g of NaOH, and 3 g of NaN_3 in sufficient water to prepare 1 liter.

c. **Sulfuric acid solution (0.18 M).** Dissolve 10 mL con (18 M H_2SO_4) in enough water to prepare 1 liter.

d. **Sodium thiosulfate solution (0.002 M).** Using a 1 liter volumetric flask, prepare a 0.10 M sodium thiosulfate stock solution by quantitatively transferring 7.9 grams sodium thiosulfate to the flask and diluting to the mark with water. Dilute this solution 50-fold (10 mL to 500 or 20 mL to 1000). For greater accuracy, the instructor may recommend that the 0.10 M stock solution may be standardized by iodometric titration against dried primary standard potassium iodate.

e. **Oxygen-saturated water.** The instructor should allow air to bubble through a reservoir containing several liters (about 1 L per student) of water for several hours prior to the beginning of lab.

f. **Oxygen-free water.** The instructor will boil a sample of water prior to the beginning of the laboratory period to drive out most of the oxygen. Oxygen-free nitrogen gas will be bubbled through the boiled water for several hours as it cools and after it reaches room temperature. This will prevent oxygen from re-entering the water and will purge any oxygen remaining after the boiling process.

g. **Starch indicator (1%).** Mix 1.0 g of starch with 10 mL of water at room temperature. Add this mixture to 100 mL boiling water and boil for a few minutes until the starch appears to be dissolved.

Special Equipment

Plastic syringe 50- or 60-mL syringe equipped with a 1-2 inch piece of transparent, flexible tubing slipped over the Luer tip.

Waste Disposal

All solutions may be rinsed down the drain with water.

Procedure

Dissolved oxygen measurement. The following steps should be followed for all dissolved oxygen measurements.

We begin by measuring dissolved oxygen in a water sample saturated with oxygen at room temperature.

Draw about 10 mL of the water sample (which has had air bubbling through it for several hours) into a large plastic syringe with short piece of tubing attached to the tip. Turn the tip of the syringe upward, tap the syringe with your finger to loosen small bubbles sticking to the plunger and the sides of the syringe, and expel the air bubbles by pushing the plunger a short way into the syringe. Then tilt the syringe downward and expel most of the water by pushing the plunger in as far as it will go. A small amount of the water sample and no bubbles should remain in the tubing attached to the syringe. Gentle pressure on the plunger should cause the liquid in the tubing to bulge outward slightly. This should be done just before dipping the tubing back into the water to collect a sample to avoid pulling air in along with the water. *There must be no air bubbles in the syringe if accurate results are to be obtained.*

Slowly draw about 32-35 mL into the syringe. Attempting to pull the liquid into the syringe too rapidly will likely cause air bubbles to form from air entering around the edges of the plunger in the syringe barrel. Carefully expel a small amount of the water until the plunger is precisely at the 30-mL mark.

Care should be taken to avoid any air bubbles as the following reagents are drawn into the syringe:

1. Draw 5 mL of manganese(II) solution into the syringe by pulling the plunger precisely to the 35-mL mark. Do not

draw more than 5 mL because the excess can not be expelled without introducing considerable error. Tilt the syringe upside down several times to cause complete mixing in the syringe.

2. Draw 5 mL of iodide solution (containing sodium hydroxide and sodium azide) into the syringe. The plunger will now be at the 40-mL mark. Again mix the solutions thoroughly for at least 2 minutes. A dark-colored precipitate of manganese(III) hydroxide will form.

3. Draw 10 mL of 0.36 N sulfuric acid into the syringe. Mix well. The manganese(III) hydroxide precipitate will disappear as iodide is oxidized to iodine. The color of the solution will range from pale yellow to brown depending on the amount of iodine formed. Once the sulfuric acid has been added, dissolved oxygen in air bubbles or in rinse water will not affect the titration because the low pH stabilizes the mixture.

A clean 50-mL buret should be set up, rinsed with 0.002 N sodium thiosulfate several times and then filled with the 0.002 N sodium thiosulfate. Air bubbles should be expelled from the buret tip and the initial buret reading recorded. When the buret with sodium thiosulfate is ready, transfer the contents of the syringe to a 125-mL erlenmeyer flask. Pull 10 or 15 mL of purified water into the syringe to rinse it and add this rinse solution to the erlenmeyer flask. Add starch indicator and titrate to the point where the blue/black starch-iodine color has just completely disappeared. Record this final buret reading.

Run a blank by using 30 mL of oxygen-free water along with all of the reagents outlined above. The number of milliliters of sodium thiosulfate solution required for the blank should be subtracted from the titration value for *all water samples tested.*

Equation VI can be used to calculate the number of grams of O_2 in the volume of water analyzed (30 mL). The number of milligrams can be calculated using equation VII:

$$O_2/mol\ S_2O_3^{2-})(L\ S_2O_3^{2-})(mol\ S_2O_3^{2-}/L)(1000\ mg/g) = mg\ O_2 \quad (VII)$$

The dissolved oxygen concentration in mg O_2 per liter is determined by dividing mg O_2 by the number of liters analyzed:

$$DO = mg\ O_2/0.030\ L \quad\quad\quad (VIII)$$

Rate of uptake of oxygen by water (option 1). Before starting this part of the experimental procedure, be prepared to begin making dissolved oxygen measurements by having the buret filled with thiosulfate solution, having at least two syringes with attached tubing ready, and having the reagents in small beakers ready for removal as needed. Pour about 500 mL of oxygen-free water into an 800-mL beaker on a magnetic stirrer and containing a magnetic stirring bar. Take a 30-mL sample as outlined above and immediately start stirring at a moderate rate which does not produce a vortex or bubbles in the water. Record the time that the stirring is begun.

Analyze the water sample in the syringe. Take DO measurements every 10 minutes for 1.5 hours. Systematically record all titration data and calculate the DO for each sample analyzed. The DO_∞ value can be assumed to be the value obtained for the oxygen-saturated water measured in the first part of the procedure.

Plot DO (mg O_2/L, y axis) as a function of time (min, x axis). On a second sheet of graph paper, plot $\ln(DO_\infty - DO_t)$ as a function of time. Calculate the slope (units should be min^{-1}) of the straight line produced by the log plot. Assuming the absorption of oxygen follows first-order kinetics, the half life is $\ln(2) \div slope$:

$$t_{1/2} = 0.693/slope \qquad \text{(IX)}$$

Biochemical Oxygen Demand (option 2). Obtain two BOD bottles from the shelf. Also obtain in a beaker about 100 mL of wastewater (untreated, primary treated, or secondary treated). The wastewater sample must not be taken after chlorination or other treatment designed to kill microorganisms. A 500-mL or 1000-mL volumetric flask is required for dilution.

A 100-fold dilution should be carried out by transferring 5.0 mL of the wastewater sample to a 500-mL volumetric flask (or 10.0 mL to 1000 mL). Dilute to the mark with oxygen-saturated water. Turn upside down to mix, and fill a BOD bottle half-way up the neck with this water. Put the ground-glass stopper in the neck of the bottle. A small amount of liquid should be displaced by the stopper into the funnel-shaped lip at the top of the bottle, and it should be allowed to remain there to prevent air entering the bottle. No air bubbles should remain in the bottle. Since the BOD bottle holds about 300 mL, some water will remain in the volumetric flask. Analyze this water for oxygen as outlined earlier. Record appropriate titration data for this sample and calculate the DO.

Prepare another sample diluted 10-fold by diluting 50 mL to 500 mL (or 100 mL to 1000 mL) in the volumetric flask. After mixing, put about 300 mL in the other BOD bottle and stopper as before so as to exclude all air bubbles and leaving a small amount of water in the funnel above the stopper. Analyze this sample for dissolved oxygen and record the data.

For a 5-day BOD determination, the bottles should be stored in an incubator for 5 days at 25°C and analyzed at the end of that time period. For student laboratories which meet only one time per week, the BOD can be estimated by allowing the bottles to stand in a dark cabinet or drawer at room temperature for one week. The samples can then be analyzed at the beginning of the next lab period.

The BOD in mg O_2/L is the difference between the initial and final dissolved-oxygen concentrations times the dilution factor:

$$\text{chemical oxygen demand} = (DO_{initial} - DO_{final}) \times (\text{dilution factor}) \ (X)$$

Waste Disposal

All solutions may be rinsed down the drain with water.

Discussion

Compare the DO obtained for oxygen saturated water to that expected at room temperature. How long would it take to achieve 97% saturation for a deoxygenated water sample stirred as in this experiment? (Hint: calculate the number of half lives required to reach approximately 97%.) How does the BOD determined in this experiment compare to that expected for this type of wastewater sample? What are the main sources of error in this experiment?

Experiment 11

Identification of Food Dyes by Paper Chromatography

General Discussion

Food dyes are commonly used in commercial products such as Kool Aid™, soft drinks, shampoo, mouthwash, toothpaste, makeup, candy, and felt tip pen ink. The purpose of these dyes is to make products more appealing so that they will be purchased by a large number of people. Dyes which are allowed in foods include the following (FD&C stands for Food, Drug, and Cosmetic):

FD&C Red 40
FD&C Yellow 5   (Tartrazine)
FD&C Yellow 6
FD&C Blue 1   (Erioglaucine)
FD&C Blue 2   (Indigo Carmine)
FD&C Green 3   (Fast Green FCF)
FD&C Red 3   (Erythrosin B)
FD&C Red 2   (Amaranth, Acid Red 27, Fast Red, Naphthol Red or Naphthylamine Red)

The latter two dyes have been used in the past but are now illegal in the U.S. in foods.

More than one dye can be added to a product. The dyes can be separated and identified by comparison with dyes of known identity. This can be done by a technique known as chromatography. In this experiment we use paper chromatography which is a fairly simple form of chromatography. With this method, a liquid solvent slowly moves along a piece of paper by capillary action. Food dyes move along with the solvent, but the movement of the dyes is slowed by intermolecular forces between the dye molecules and the paper. Each dye moves at its own particular rate with some moving considerably faster than others. The rates of movement of various dyes can be compared by using their R_f values. An R_f value for a dye in a given solvent is a ratio between how far the dye moves and how far the solvent moves in the same period of time.

$$R_f = \frac{\text{distance dye moves in a given time}}{\text{distance solvent moves in the same time}}$$

Reagents and Special Apparatus

a. **Ethanol.**

b. **Petri Dishes (9 cm diameter).**

c. **Capillary (melting point) Tubes.**

d. **Small vials of pure, solid dyes:** FD&C Red 40, FD&C Yellow 5, FD&C Yellow 6, FD&C Blue 1, FD&C Blue 2, FD&C Green 3, FD&C Red 3, FD&C Red 2.

e. **Filter paper (11 cm).**

Procedure

1. Preparation of developing solution. Prepare 50% ethanol/50% water (v/v) by mixing 25 mL each of water and ethanol in a small beaker or flask. Put about 15 mL of this solution in each of three Petri dishes and place the cover over each dish.

2. Preparation of "known" dye solutions. Dissolve a small amount (about the size of a match head) of each of the eight dyes in separate 1-mL portions of ethanol in test tubes. It will later be necessary to transfer the contents of each of these test tubes to beakers or watch glasses to "spot" the chromatography paper.

3. Preparation of chromatograms. Cut three pieces of Whatman #1 filter paper (11 cm) as illustrated in the figure at the top of the next page. Fold the strip at the center and leave as the wick. The first two papers will be used for the "known" dyes (4 on each paper) and will include (1) red 2, (2) red 40, (3) blue 1, (4) blue 2, (5) yellow 5, and (6) yellow 6, (7) red 3, and (8) green 3. The other paper will be used for Kool Aid™ "unknowns" which will include (1) cherry, (2) grape, and/or (3) lime flavors and for inks from green or black Flair™ felt-tip pens.

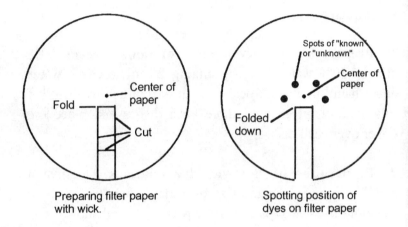

Preparing filter paper with wick.

Spotting position of dyes on filter paper

On the first paper you will make four spots for the first four "knowns" and on the second paper you will make four more spots for the last four "knowns". The third piece of filter paper will have two spots of colored solution from candy or artificially colored drinks and two spots from felt-tip pens. These spots should be as small as possible. A diameter of no more than 3 mm is best. You may have to try several pieces of paper until you come up with one which is evenly spotted around the center with **small** spots. **Circle each spot with a <u>pencil</u> and number each on the paper. Do not use a pen or the ink will interfere with the chromatography.**

The developing solution should already be in the bottoms of three 9-cm petri dishes. Place the spotted filter papers on top of the dish bottoms with only the wick in the developing solution. Place the petri dish covers over the filter papers and push down so that the cover tightly crimps the paper in place in the dish. Only the wick should be in the developing solution. Allow these to sit undisturbed for one hour or until the paper looks wet toward the outside edge of the petri dish. While the chromatograms are developing, the instructors will demonstrate various kinds of other chromatographic techniques.

4. Analysis of the chromatogram. When the liquid developing solvent has moved to where it is near the outer edge of the petri dish, remove the cover and quickly, before the solvent evaporates, draw a circle with a pencil following the wet circle on the paper produced by the solvent. This is called the solvent front. Do this for both the known and unknown papers.

After the paper has dried, record the following data on the report sheet.

Measure the distance in centimeters between the center of the initial spotting position (for each spot) and the center of the spot after it has moved during development of the chromatogram. This is the "distance the spot has moved". Then measure the distance from the center of the initial spotting position of each spot and the solvent front. This is the "distance the solvent has moved". Calculate the R_f value for each known dye and for each unknown dye in the three Kool Aids^{TM}.

$$R_f = \frac{dis\tan ce \text{ the solute moved}}{dis\tan ce \text{ the solvent moved}}$$

Compare the R_f values of the unknown dyes to those of the knowns and use this information to identify the Kool Aid dyes.

Waste Disposal

All solutions may be rinsed down the drain with water.

Report the Following Data:

Dyes with Known Identity

Number of spot	Name of dye	Distance spot moved	Distance solvent moved	R_f value

Unknown Dyes

me of l Aid™ r Pen	Color of spot	Distance spot moved	Distance solvent moved	R_f value	Identity of spot

Molecular Models

One of the most difficult aspects of learning about the structures of organic molecules is visualizing the arrangement of atoms and the shapes of the many linear, branched, cyclic, aromatic, and polycyclic compounds which are possible. The possibility of numerous isomeric structures and of many functional groups just adds to the confusion. The purpose of this experiment is simply to allow students to construct 3-dimensional models of common organic molecules and some which are less common but of environmental significance. The experiment covers the structures of simple aliphatic straight-chain and branched hydrocarbons, cycloalkanes, aromatic hydrocarbons, halogenated organic compounds, and oxygen-containing organic compounds.

Students should work in groups of 2 and prepare models as directed by the experimental directions. These models should be kept until the instructor has had an opportunity to examine each and put an "ok" in the laboratory notebook. It is a very good idea to have the laboratory notebook set up before coming to the lab so that names, formulas, and structures can be recorded in a neat, logical format, and to save time. It is also essential that the student bring the textbook to use as a reference during this lab exercise.

Procedure

After recording a short description of the experimental objective and the procedure, **set up the lab notebook pages in a table format with room to record (1) the formula, (2) the name, and (3) the line structure of each compound for which a model is prepared.** Be sure to get the instructor's "ok" on each compound studied. Whenever a question is asked in the directions, be sure to answer the question in the notebook in a place where the answer can be easily found by the reader.

The model kits come with various colors to represent a variety of atoms.

Hydrogen: white   carbon: black
chlorine: green   oxygen: red
bromine, iodine, fluorine: use any other colors available

Prepare models, get the instructor's "ok", and record (1) the formula, (2) the name, and (3) the structural formula (using lines to connect bonded atoms):

1. **Alkanes.**
   a. n-Propane (are any branched structures possible?)
   b. All isomers (branched and straight-chain) of C_4H_{10}
   c. All isomers (branched and straight-chain) of C_5H_{12}

2. **Cycloalkanes.**
   a. cyclohexane
      Cyclohexane has "chair" and "boat" forms; what does this mean?
   b. cyclobutane
   c. cyclopropane
      Why do you think cyclopropane and cyclobutane molecules are less stable than cyclohexane?

3. **Alkenes.**
   a. propene
   b. cis-2-butene
   c. trans-2-butene
      Why are cis and trans isomers of 1-butene not possible?

4. **Aromatic Compounds.**
   a. benzene
   b. naphthalene
   c. biphenyl
   d. pyridine (C_5H_5N)
   e. pentachlorophenol ("penta" wood preservative)

5. **Halogenated Compounds.**
   a. dichlorodifluoromethane (freon-12)
   b. bromochlorofluoroiodomethane
      There are two "stereoisomers" of this compound. See if you can construct models of each of them.
   c. HFC-134 (there are two isomers)
   d. any polychlorinated biphenyl
   e. DDT (dichlorodiphenyltrichloroethane)

6. **Other Functional Groups.**
   a. two isomers with the formula C_2H_6O
   b. two isomers with the formula C_3H_6O

7. **Molecular models as learning tools.**
   At the end of the notebook write-up of this experiment include a discussion of the usefulness of molecular models in understanding various aspects of organic structure. In what way(s) do model kits make structure more understandable?

Identification of FD&C Dyes by Visible Spectrophotometry

(a modification of McKone and Ivie, *J. Chem. Educ.*, **57** 1980, 321-322
and Ondrus and Brice, *J. Chem. Educ.*, **62** 1985, 798-799)

General Discussion

All artificially colored foods in the United States are tinted with a relatively small number of synthetic (coal-tar derived) dyes. The most commonly used dyes include food, drug, and cosmetic (FD&C) Yellow 5, Red 3, Blue 1, Red 40, Orange B (only allowed in casings of sausage and similar meats), and Citrus Red 2 (only allowed on orange skins). Other allowed FD&C dyes include Yellow 6, Blue 2, and Green 3. Presently, Red 2 and Red 4 are banned, but they were used in some foods such as maraschino cherries until about 15 years ago. Red 2 (banned in 1976 because of evidence indicating that it may increase the likelihood of cancer) is considered by many color chemists to produce a red which for many applications is esthetically more pleasing than the currently accepted Red 40.

At present, manufacturers of materials containing FD&C dyes are not required to list on the label the specific dye or dyes used. They may simply use the term "artificial color", but many products are now indicating the color which is actually used. We will identify FD&C dye or dyes in at least one food product from their absorption maxima by comparing with the information provided in Table 1. Dyes will be separated and isolated for spectrophotometric identification by solvent gradient chromatography by means of simple liquid chromatography with a disposable liquid chromatography cartridge.

This experiment demonstrates a simple chromatographic separation which is easy to visualize due to the brilliant colors produced by FD&C dyes. Detection and identification is aided by use of a spectrophotometer which can sense wavelength and color intensity variations with greater precision than the human eye. The procedure is **qualitative** in that it allows one to determine the identity of an unknown dye in a commercial product. **Quantitative** methods allow the analyst to determine the amount of a substance present, and that is not done in this experiment.

Materials

a. **10-mL plastic or glass syringe.**

b. **syringe-adaptable C18 "Sep Pak" liquid chromatography cartridge (Millipore/Waters).**

c. **Methanol.**

d. **FD&C dyes or dye solutions (Red 3, Red 40, Yellow 5, Yellow 6, Blue 1, Blue 2, Green 3).**

e. **Artificially colored food** such as strawberry, cherry, or grape Kool Aid™; grape soda; red, green, yellow, or purple Lifesaver candies; or **felt-tip pens** (such as green or black Papermate "Flair™") with water-soluble inks.

Instrumentation

A rapid-scanning spectrophotometer such as the modern UV-visible photodiode array instruments with printer or plotter is preferred. The time required to extract and separate dyes is less than one hour. This leaves a good deal of time for recording spectra with a scanning instrument.

Waste Disposal

All solutions may be rinsed down the drain with water.

Procedure

Known Dyes. Prepare solutions of dyes such as Yellow 5, Red 40, and Blue 1 (the instructor will indicate which dyes to use) by dissolving a drop of the concentrated dye solution or a **very minute amount of the solid** in 200 mL of water. Absorption spectra of these two or three "knowns" should be run to allow comparison of experimentally measured absorption maxima and absorption maxima predicted in Table 1.

Foods Containing Unknown Dyes. Artificially colored candy, other food products, or pens containing water soluble dyes will be provided by the instructor. Separate the dyes in Kool Aid™ (or similar artificially colored products) using a procedure similar to that suggested in the following paragraphs.

Prepare a "Sep Pak" by passing 5 mL of methanol through it with a syringe. Then rinse the "Sep Pak" with 5 mL of water from a syringe.

The dyes in the unknown mixture must first be isolated or separated from each other by chromatography. If a colored candy product is being studied, grind 5 - 10 grams to a powder with a mortar and pestle. Transfer the powdered product to 10 - 15 mL warm water to dissolve. If felt-tip pen ink is being analyzed, stir the tip of the pen in 5 mL water for 5 seconds. If a soft drink or other artificially colored liquid is being studied, no pretreatment or dilution is necessary. Draw 2 - 4 mL of the colored solution into a 10-mL syringe. Then attach a Sep Pak to the syringe and force the colored mixture through the cartridge slowly allowing the liquid to pass into a test tube.

Set up a series of 8 more test tubes for isolating the dye or dyes.

Remove the cartridge from the syringe, rinse the syringe with water, and then refill it with 9 mL H_2O and 1 mL methanol. Replace the cartridge on the syringe and slowly force the H_2O - methanol mixture through it. Run the first 5 mL of this mixture in the second test tube. Run the remaining 5 mL of this mixture into a third test tube. If two or more dyes are present, one of them may have begun separating by this time. Repeat this procedure, allowing 5 mL of the next solution to run into the fourth test tube and the second 5 mL to run into the fifth tube.

When the first dye appears to have been completely eluted from the chromatography cartridge, use 10 mL of an 8-mL H_2O/2-mL methanol mixture to begin eluting the second dye into a new test tube. Follow this with a 7-mL H_2O/3-mL methanol mixture, a 6-mL H_2O/4-mL methanol mixture, and finally a 5-mL methanol/5-mL H_2O mixture, running the first 5 mL of each new 10 mL mixture into a test tube and the second 5 mL into another clean test tube. (Rinse the chromatography cartridge with pure methanol followed by water before reuse.)

Pick the test tubes which appear to have the purest most concentrated solution of the dyes and run their spectra as outlined in the following procedure. If you or your instructor are not satisfied with the way the dyes have separated, try repeating the procedure.

Absorption Spectra

Scanning spectrophotometer. The spectra of all standard solutions may be determined directly by placing several milliliters of each in the sample cuvette in a scanning spectrophotometer. Use purified water as a reference. Scan from 400 to 800 nm. If desired, all standard spectra may be overlaid on the same plot to be handed in with the report sheet. If a scanning instrument is available for a group of 2 to 4 students, all data can be collected, and results turned in, in 2 to 3 hours.

Fixed Wavelength Spectrophotometer. An alternate method of obtaining absorption spectra consists of measuring the absorbance of the dye solution at a series of wavelengths with a Spectronic 20, Spectronic 21, or similar spectrophotometer and then plotting the data on a piece of graph paper. **This is a slow procedure and will take the remainder of a lab period to collect the data. The graphing of the data, described below, may be done outside the lab or during another lab period.** Use two matched cells (cuvettes) filling one with deionized water and the other with the dye solution to be analyzed. Set the wavelength of the instrument at 400 nm, and, using the "blank" (deionized water) cuvette adjust the instrument to an absorbance reading of 0.00. Then put the dye-containing cuvette into the cell compartment, and measure the absorbance. When this measurement is done, increase the wavelength by 25 nanometers to 425 nm. Repeat the "zeroing" procedure with the "blank" cuvette, and measure the absorbance of the dye solution. Continue increasing the wavelength in 25 nm increments, zeroing, and measuring the dye absorbance up to 800 nm. Then go back to the *wavelength range* of 25 to 50 nm over which the absorbance values were the strongest. Take absorbance readings every 5 nm over this range. Be sure to zero the absorbance reading before each measurement using a blank. Record all data on the report sheet.

If data points have been collected with a fixed wavelength spectrophotometer, label the x axis of a piece of graph paper "wavelength", and subdivide this axis so that the 400 - 800 nm visible light range covers the full amount of graph paper space available. The y axis should be labeled "absorbance" and should run from 0.00 at the origin to a maximum which is a bit higher than the highest absorbance reading measured. Data points for two or three standards can be plotted in different colors to allow several curves to be put on the same piece of graph paper. It is recommended that "knowns" be plotted on one piece of paper and "unknowns" on a second paper. For each dye, a **smooth curve** should be drawn through the data points. A curve drawing tool such as a French curve may be helpful to do this. **Do not** connect successive data points with straight-line segments.

Waste Disposal

All dye solutions and solvents may be rinsed down the drain with water.

Data Analysis

Use the absorption curve obtained from the spectrophotometer or plotted by hand to estimate the approximate wavelength at which a maximum absorbance level is reached, and record this as the "observed" absorption maximum on the report sheet. Use Table 1 to identify the "expected" absorption maximum for each of the knowns and record this value on the report sheet. Using the spectra of the unknown dyes in the commercial product(s) identify each dye from its observed absorption maximum after consulting Table 1. Attach all spectra to the report sheet.

Draw the structure of each dye (and name it) that was detected in a commercial food or beverage.

Table 1: Expected Absorption Maxima (nm) of FD&C Dyes		
Dye	Solvent System	Absorption Maxima[a](nm)
Yellow 5	water	422
Yellow 6	water	480
Red 4	water	495
Red 40	water	505
Red 2	water	520
Red 3	water	527
Blue 2	water	610
Green 3	water	625
Blue 1	water	627

[a] The maxima will vary slightly due to variations in solvent and spectrophotometer operation.

The chemical structures of FD&C dyes are given on the next two pages:

Red 4

Red 2

Red 3

Yellow 6

Yellow 5

Red 40

Blue 1

Blue 2

Green 3

Report the following data:

Turn in all absorption spectra - Known Dyes and the Unknown Dyes from the food, beverage, or other sample. Be sure to identify each spectrum with respect to the known or unknown dye which it represents.

Knowns Names	Expected Absorption Maxima	Observed Absorption Maxima
_____	_____	_____
_____	_____	_____
_____	_____	_____
_____	_____	_____

Sample Identity	Observed Absorption Maxima	Identity of Dye
1. _____	_____	_____
2. _____	_____	_____

Discussion

What evidence supports your identification of dyes in the commercial product?

Is there any evidence which indicates that one or more of your identifications may be incorrect?

Write the names and draw the chemical structures of all dyes identified in commercial foods or beverages by you and your lab partner(s).

Detection of Fuel Components by Gas Chromatography

General Discussion

In this experiment we take advantage of the high resolving power and rapidity of gas chromatography to separate some commercial liquid fuels into individual compounds or simple mixtures of compounds of similar volatility.

Table 2 lists the major components of a typical commercial gasoline. Their order of appearance in a gas chromatographic separation is determined both by their volatility and by their polarity, which, determines their interaction with the column's stationary phase. In gas chromatography retention time is often related directly to boiling point.

The location of an individual compound in a gas chromatogram can be established by injecting the pure compound and determining the elution time for that component. That peak can then be identified in a fuel chromatogram by locating the peak with the same elution time. Individual components can also be located by addition of known compounds to the gasoline and comparison of peak height in "spiked" and "unspiked" samples.

The composition of a fuel influences its combustion properties. A poorly formulated gasoline causes engine knocking and poor combustion. Knocking is caused by fuels with a low octane rating. Normal alkanes have a low octane rating (n-heptane = 0), branched paraffins inter-mediate ratings ("isooctane", 2,2,4-trimethylpentane = 100), and aromatics have high octane numbers (toluene = 103). Small amounts of tetraethyl lead (3-4 cc/gal) enhance the octane ratings of gasoline but produce some environmental problems. Unfortunately caution must be used in replacing tetraethyl lead with aromatics because of the toxicity of some aromatic hydrocarbons. The purpose of this experiment is to use a gas chromatograph (GC) to separate and identify several of the most common hydrocarbons which are found in gasoline. The data is used to determine the approximate percent composition of certain hydrocarbons which are commonly used to improve the octane rating of a fuel.

Reagents: The following three fuels: Regular gasoline, Premium unleaded gasoline, Unleaded gasoline. The following pure compounds: n-pentane, n-hexane, n-heptane, n-octane, n-nonane, benzene, toluene, xylene (mixture of o-, m-, and p-), and 2,2,4-trimethylpentane (isooctane).

Typical Instrumentation: Hewlett Packard 5890 A Gas Chromatograph equipped with a 10-meter, 0.53-mm ID methyl-silicone-gum coated (2.53 mm film thickness) glass column, thermal conductivity detector, and 3393 A Integrator. The integrator is necessary if % total peak area is to be used to approximate percent composition of hydrocarbons in gasoline.

Instrument Settings

Equilibrium Time = 0.50 min   Instrument Range = 0
Detector = thermal conductivity 120 °C   Instrument Attenuation = 0
Injector temperature = 150 °C   Integrator Attenuation = 4
Initial Oven Temperature = 30 °C   Peak width = 0.02
Initial Time = 1.00 min   Chart Speed = 2.0 cm/min
Rate = 20 °C/min   Area Rejection = 2000
Final Temp = 90 °C   Threshold = 0
Final Time = 3.00 min

Procedure

Arrange 11 small (25-mL) flasks and label them 1-11. Place in the flasks the following:

Flask	Contents
1	2 mL regular gasoline
2	2 mL unleaded gasoline
3	2 mL premium unleaded
4	2 mL n-pentane plus 2 drops n-nonane
5	2 mL n-pentane plus 2 drops n-octane
6	2 mL n-pentane plus 2 drops n-heptane
7	2 mL n-pentane plus 2 drops n-hexane
8	2 mL n-pentane plus 2 drops toluene
9	2 mL n-pentane plus 2 drops xylene
10	2 mL n-pentane plus 2 drops isooctane
11	2 mL n-pentane plus 2 drops benzene

Inject a 1.0-µL sample. The instructor will demonstrate proper injection technique and operation of the instrumentation.

The "standard" samples (flasks 4-11) are designed to allow the identification of various gasoline components in

113

the chromatogram. Each standard will have a large peak for pentane and a smaller peak (or peaks) for the compound that was added to the pentane. Retention times for all known compounds will be determined and recorded.

Rinse flasks with n-propyl alcohol (not water) when all samples have been run.

Waste Disposal

All unused gasoline and flask rinsings should be poured into the nonhalogenated organic solvent waste receptacle.

Analysis of Data

Record the retention time of each "known" hydrocarbon. Using the retention times of the standards, identify known peaks on the three fuel chromatograms (flasks 1-3).

It is possible to estimate the relative amount of a component by comparing the % peak area of a hydrocarbon in different gasoline samples. The sample with the highest % peak area has the greatest amount of that component. Use the chromatograms obtained from flask 1, 2, and 3 to determine the % peak area for isooctane, benzene, toluene, and xylene. Record these values.

Which fuel(s) contain(s) the most benzene, toluene, xylene, and isooctane, and which contain(s) the least? Why?

Also, record the retention times of n-pentane, n-hexane, n-heptane, n-octane, n-nonane, isooctane, benzene, toluene, and xylene. Use the Handbook of Chemistry and Physics to find the boiling point of each of these hydrocarbons. How are retention time and boiling point related?

Major Hydrocarbons in Gasoline

Aliphatic Hydrocarbons	Formula	Octane Number
n-pentane	$CH_3-CH_2-CH_2-CH_2-CH_3$	62
n-hexane	$CH_3-CH_2-CH_2-CH_2-CH_2-CH_3$	25
n-heptane	$CH_3-CH_2-CH_2-CH_2-CH_2-CH_2-CH_3$	0
n-octane	$CH_3-CH_2-CH_2-CH_2-CH_2-CH_2-CH_2-CH_3$	-19
1-pentene	$CH_2{=}CH-CH_2-CH_2-CH_3$	91

methylcyclopentane

2,2-dimethylhexane $\quad CH_3-\overset{\overset{\textstyle CH_3}{|}}{\underset{\underset{\textstyle CH_3}{|}}{C}}-CH_2-CH_2-CH_2-CH_3 \qquad 93$

2,4-dimethylhexane $\quad CH_3-\overset{\overset{\textstyle CH_3}{|}}{CH}-CH_2-\overset{\overset{\textstyle CH_3}{|}}{CH}-CH_2-CH_3 \qquad 65$

2,2,4 trimethylpentane
(isooctane) $\quad CH_3-\overset{\overset{\textstyle CH_3}{|}}{\underset{\underset{\textstyle CH_3}{|}}{C}}-CH_2-\overset{\overset{\textstyle CH_3}{|}}{CH}-CH_3 \qquad 100$

Aromatic Hydrocarbons	Structure	Octane Number
benzene		106
toluene		103
o-xylene		107
m-xylene		118
p-xylene		116

Alcohols	Formula	Octane Number
Methanol	CH_3-OH	116
Ethanol	CH_3-CH_2-OH	112

Report the Following data:

Identify the Fuels Studied.

Attach chromatograms of three fuels with known peaks
labeled as to their identity.

	Boiling Points	Retention Times
n-pentane		
n-hexane		
n-heptane		
n-octane		
n-nonane		
benzene		
isooctane		
toluene		
xylene		

**Discuss the relationship between retention time and
boiling point.**

nzene % of Total Peak Area
1.
2.
3.

Toluene % of Total Peak Area
1.
2.
3.

lene % of Total Peak Area
1.
2.
3.

Isooctane % of Total Peak Area
1.
2.
3.

Fuel with greatest amount of isooctane: _____

Fuel with least amount of isooctane: _____

Fuel with greatest amount of total xylenes: _____

Fuel with least amount of total xylenes: _____

Fuel with greatest amount of toluene: _____

Fuel with least amount of toluene: _____

Explain the variation in the above four hydrocarbons in these fuel blends:

Determination of Heat of Combustion of Coal Using Bomb Calorimetry

General Discussion

When fuels are burned, the products of the oxidation are carbon dioxide and water. If the fuel contains sulfur, nitrogen, or metal compounds, some oxides of these elements, such as sulfur dioxide, are also produced.

In bomb calorimetry, a combustible mixture is burned in a pure oxygen environment in a heavy, stainless-steel vessel called a "bomb". The heat released in the reaction causes the water reservoir surrounding the bomb to increase in temperature. The total amount of energy released during the combustion of a sample (kcal/g) can be determined simply by multiplying the change in temperature of the calorimeter system (°C) times the heat capacity of the calorimeter system (kcal/°C) and dividing by the number of grams of sample used.

$$\text{t of combustion of a fuel} = \frac{(\Delta T)(\text{heat capacity of system})}{(\text{wt of sample})} \qquad (I)$$

The heat capacity of the calorimeter (units of kcal/°C) is the combination of the heat capacity of the bomb, the water surrounding the bomb, the stirrer, the thermometer and the water container. However the heat capacity is determined quite simply by running a standard (benzoic acid) which has a known heat of combustion of 6.32 kcal/g and rearranging equation I to produce equation II.

$$(\text{heat capacity of system}) = \frac{(6.32 \text{ kcal} / \text{g})(\text{wt of benzoic acid used})}{(\Delta T)}$$

Materials

Volumetric flasks (2000-mL, 1000-mL, and 200-mL); a plastic beaker or bucket to hold water, an insulating container around the bucket; a water agitator; benzoic acid; anthracite, lignite and bituminous coal samples.

Instrumentation

Parr 1108 oxygen combustion bomb; bomb-head support stand; digital thermometer and thermocouple with 0.01° C precision; oxygen cylinder with oxygen regulator; ignition unit and 10-cm fuse wire; hydraulic press; pellet die.

Procedure

1. Use three volumetric flasks (2000-mL, 1000-mL, and 200-mL) to dispense 3200 mL of water into the plastic water reservoir of the calorimeter.

2. Place about 1.1 g of benzoic acid in the pellet die, and apply very light pressure with the hydraulic press to produce a pellet.

3. Transfer the pellet to the tared combustion cup and weigh on an analytical balance and record the weight of the cup, the cup plus the pellet, and, by subtraction, the benzoic acid in the pellet to the nearest 0.0001 g. Be careful not to chip the pellet so that none of the sample is lost. **Note:** the powdered sample is pelletized to ensure that all of it will burn once combustion is started.

4. Put the bomb head in the support stand. Measure approximately 10 cm of fuse wire, and thread the two ends through the holes in the two electrodes on the bomb head. (See Figure 1.) Press down the two locking caps to secure the wire to the two electrodes.

5. Place the combustion cup plus the pellet in the electrode loop. The fuse wire is then shaped so that it dips down and touches the sample pellet but does not touch the sides of the metal cup. (See Figure 1.)

6. Remove the bomb head from the support stand, and place it on the bomb body being careful not to disturb the pellet or the fuse wire. Screw the cap onto the bomb and tighten by hand. (See Figure 1.)

7. Place the O_2-hose slip connector on the fitting of the bomb head. Purge the bomb three times at 20 atm with oxygen. Then fill the bomb to 30 atm with oxygen.

Release the line pressure using the line purge lever (Figure 2).

8. Place the bomb in the center of the water bath. If bubbles are being produced, the bomb is leaking, and the procedure should be stopped with the bomb being resealed and repressurized.

9. Lower the stirrer (water agitator) into the water around the bomb. Place the cover on the calorimeter with the ignition wires being threaded through the hole in the cover and inserted into the terminals of the bomb.

10. Thread the thermocouple through the cover opening into the water. Be careful that it will not be disturbed by the motion of the agitator. See Figure 3 for the overall setup.

11. Record the steady temperature of the water. Press the black button on the ignition unit for three seconds. The red indicator light should flash on momentarily and the temperature of the system should begin to rise. *If there is no temperature change, the fuse wire will have to be checked and possibly replaced.*

12. Mix the water slowly with the agitator.

13. Monitor the temperature of the system until it reaches a steady level after 5-10 minutes.

14. Remove the bomb from the calorimeter and open the purge valve on the calorimeter. When the pressure has been released, open the bomb and place the head in the

support stand. Remove any remaining fuse wire from the electrodes.

The above procedure should be repeated at least two times with benzoic acid to determine the heat capacity of the calorimeter. The procedure should then be used to run coal samples with a minimum of two runs per coal or fuel sample. If the coal is in the form of solid pieces, it is not necessary to prepare a pellet. Instead, a single "chunk" weighing 1.0 to 1.5 g should be used. If a powdered coal sample is used, it should be pressed into a pellet because a pellet will ignite more reliably than a loose powder. Record all weights and all temperature changes observed.

Calculations

Use the data from the benzoic acid runs to calculate the mean heat capacity of the calorimeter. Then calculate the heat of combustion of each coal or fuel sample using the mean heat capacity of the calorimeter and the measured temperature change in the system. Finally calculate the number of kcal per gram and Btu per pound of each kind of coal.

How do these results compare with accepted or anticipated values? What is/are the biggest source(s) of error in this procedure?

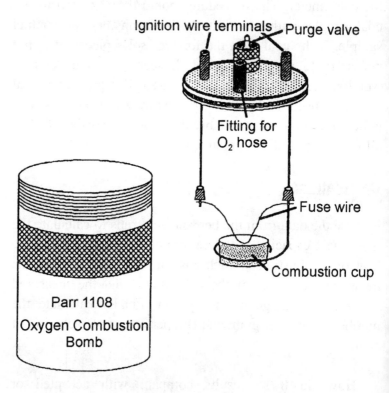

Figure 1. Location of components on bomb head

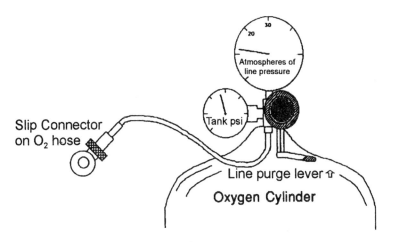

Slip Connector
on O_2 hose

Figure 2. Oxygen cylinder with regulator and hose connectors.

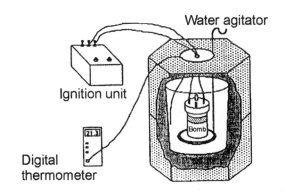

Figure 3. Overall calorimeter setup

Heat of Combustion
and
Efficiency of Heat Transfer

General Discussion

The words heat and temperature are often confusingly used interchangeably and incorrectly. Temperature is a measure of how hot or how cold an object is and it is measured in degrees Fahrenheit or Celsius. Heat, on the other hand, is a measure of what makes objects get hot and is measured in calories (cal). These calories are similar to, but not exactly the same as, the calories you count when you're on a diet.

The purpose of this experiment is to approximate the heat of combustion of paraffin wax in a candle by measuring the heat absorbed from the burning candle by a known amount of water, to compare the measured value to the "known" heat of combustion of candle wax, and to calculate the efficiency of heating water with a candle.

Materials

Small candles such as birthday or votive candles work nicely. An alcohol lamp or a butane lighter may be substituted for the candle.

Instrumentation

Analytical balance precise to the nearest 1 or 0.1 milligram; thermometer; small metal can such a soup, juice, or soft-drink can.

Procedure

From the reagent shelf, obtain a small candle. Determine the total weight of the candle to the nearest 0.001 or 0.0001 gram.

Obtain a small steel can, measure and record the weight of the can, and pour 100 mL of water into it. Measure and record the initial temperature of the water (plus can) in degrees Celsius.

Place the candle under the can of water on a ring stand. The can should be placed on a wire triangle on a ring stand and the candle should be positioned under the can so that the tip of the flame will be just under the bottom surface of the can. Strike a kitchen match and light the candle.

After the temperature of the water has increased by about 20°, extinguish the flame and record the final temperature of the heated water. Subtract the initial temperature from the final temperature; this is the temperature change.

Allow the unburned candle wax to cool to room temperature and solidify. Reweigh the candle to determine the weight of fuel consumed.

Calculations

Look up the specific heats of water and iron (we will assume that the steel can is composed primarily of iron). Use these values, and the masses of water and of the can to calculate the number of calories of heat provided by the candle which was absorbed by the water plus the container.

Heat absorbed = (g H_2O)(sp. ht. H_2O)(ΔT) + (g Fe)(sp. ht. Fe)(ΔT)

This is less than the number of calories of heat given off by the burning of the fuel because some heat is lost to the surroundings. Divide this number of calories by the total weight in grams of the wax consumed during burning. This gives you the number of calories absorbed by the water/can system per gram of fuel .

Since 1000 calories (1000 cal) is equal to 1 kilocalorie (1 kcal) and 1000 grams (1000 g) is equal to one kilogram (1 kg), the number of calories per gram is equal to the number of kilocalories per kilogram of fuel. One Btu is equal to 0.252 kcal and 454 g is equal to 1 lb. Convert to British thermal units per pound (Btu/lb).

Repeat this experiment two more times.

Candle wax consists of moderately high molecular weight alkanes (paraffins) of which n-eicosane is a typical example. Look up the heat of combustion of eicosane ($C_{20}H_{42}$). Compare the literature value for the heat of combustion of this compound to the corresponding value for candle wax determined in this experiment. Calculate the percent efficiency of heat transfer.

% efficiency = (experimental value/literature value)(100)

Report the Following Data: Weight of can = ____ g

Data	Exp 1	Exp 2	Exp 3
Volume of water in can	___ mL	___ mL	___ mL
Initial weight of candle	__ g	__ g	__ g
Weight of candle after heating	__ g	__ g	__ g
Weight of wax consumed	__ g	__ g	__ g
Initial temperature of water + can	__ °C	__ °C	__ °C
Final temperature of water + can	__°C	__°C	__ °C
Temperature change of water + can	__ °C	__ °C	__ °C

Calculations

	Exp 1	Exp 2	Exp 3
Calculated number of calories absorbed by the water + can	___ cal	___ cal	___ cal
Number of calories per gram of fuel	___ cal/g	___ cal/g	___ cal/g
Number of kilocalories per kilogram of fuel	__ kcal/kg	__kcal/kg	__ kcal/kg
Number of British thermal units per pound of fuel	___ Btu/lb	___ Btu/lb	___ Btu/lb

Discussion

Heat of combustion of eicosane from literature
_____ Btu/lb
Calculated efficiency of transfer of heat from burning
candle to water _____ %

Note: Calculate the efficiency by dividing the heat of combustion determined in this experiment by the literature value and then multiplying this fraction by 100.

Measurement of Sulfur Content in Coal

(a modification of Koubek and Stewart,
J. Chem. Educ., **69** 1992, A146-A148)

General Discussion

Coal has been an important energy source since the mid-1800s. Although there are several sub-varieties, coal is usually one of three types: anthracite (hard coal), bituminous (soft coal), and lignite (brown coal). Anthracite contains the highest percent carbon, has the highest heating value, is usually low in sulfur content, and is fairly rare. Bituminous is fairly common both in the environment and in its use, but it is generally fairly high in sulfur with an average of 2 - 3 percent sulfur by weight.

A 1.7 megawatt electricity generating plant is likely to burn from 600 to 650 tons of bituminous coal, containing about 2.5% sulfur, per hour. If no sulfur oxide removal equipment is installed, such a plant will oxidize 15 tons of sulfur per hour potentially leading to the production of up to 1100 tons of sulfuric acid in the environment each day.

Coal samples for this experiment are readily available from local utility companies and in some cases from college or university heating plants if coal is the primary energy source. Usually the plant operator can provide a fairly accurate estimate of the sulfur content of the coal for comparison to results obtained by students.

In this experiment, sulfur in coal is converted to water-soluble sulfate by heating the coal overnight in an 800° muffle furnace with a mixture of MgO and Na_2CO_3. The reactions that take place may be represented by the following equations:

$$S_{\text{(as organic sulfur compounds and metal sulfides)}} + O_2 \longrightarrow SO_2$$

$$Na_2CO_3 \cdot MgO + SO_2 + 1/2 O_2 \longrightarrow Na_2SO_4 + MgO + CO_2$$

The soluble sulfate is dissolved in water and precipitated as barium sulfate by adding barium chloride solution. The solid barium sulfate is then recovered by filtration, washed to remove soluble salts, and dissolved in EDTA solution. Barium sulfate is extremely insoluble in water, but EDTA solubilizes it because the barium ion chelates strongly with EDTA. The uncomplexed EDTA is then titrated with standard magnesium chloride solution. By subtracting the moles of $MgCl_2$ added from the total moles of EDTA used, the moles of sulfur and percent sulfur in the coal sample can be determined.

The purpose of this experiment is to determine the percent sulfur in a coal sample by titration. The coal sample is first ignited in a muffle furnace to convert the sulfur to sulfate ion. The sulfur is recovered in the form of solid barium sulfate, dissolved in excess EDTA solution, and determined indirectly by titration of the excess EDTA with standard magnesium chloride solution.

Note

The coal samples used in this experiment should be prepared and placed in the muffle furnace at the end of the preceding experiment. They will then be ready for analysis the following laboratory period. Analysis will generally take two laboratory periods.

Materials

a. **MgO/Na$_2$CO$_3$ Mixture.** Mix two parts by weight MgO and 1 part Na$_2$CO$_3$.

b. **6 M HCl.**

c. **Barium chloride solution, ca. 0.05 M.** Prepare from the reagent-grade salt.

d. **EDTA solution, 0.05 M.** Dissolve 18.613 g of disodium dihydrogen ethylenediaminetetraacetate dihydrate (dried at 80° C, MW 372.25) in deionized water and dilute to 1.00 liter in a volumetric flask.

e. **Magnesium chloride solution, *ca.* 0.05 M.** Weigh to the nearest 0.1 mg 0.28 - 0.30 g of magnesium turnings, dissolve in a little 2 M HCl, and dilute with deionized water to 250 mL in a volumetric flask. Calculate the exact concentration from the weight of magnesium used.

f. Buffer solution, pH = 10. Add 57 mL of concentrated ammonia solution to 7.0 g of ammonium chloride and dilute to 100 mL.

g. Eriochrome Black T indicator. Dissolve 0.2 g of the dye in 15 mL triethanolamine and 5 mL absolute ethanol.

Instrumentation

Muffle furnace, burets, vacuum filtration units, Whatman #1 and Whatman #42 filter paper, magnetic stirring hot plate, mortar and pestle.

Procedure

Weigh, in triplicate, 1 g samples of powdered coal in clean porcelain crucibles. It may be necessary to pulverize the coal with a mortar and pestle. Record the weight of each coal sample to four decimal places. Add approximately 3 g of Na_2CO_3/MgO mixture to each coal sample in each crucible. Use a spatula to thoroughly mix the powdered coal and the Na_2CO_3/MgO. When the spatula is removed, it should be tapped against the inside of the crucible to remove any of the coal which may be sticking to the spatula. Then each crucible should be lightly tapped on the desk surface to flatten and pack the mixture in the crucible. Add another gram of Na_2CO_3/MgO mixture to each crucible to cover the coal mixture, cover the crucibles, and place them in an 800° C muffle furnace for a minimum of 12 hours. Several days would be okay. The absence of black particles after heating indicates complete reaction.

When the crucibles have cooled to room temperature, transfer the entire contents of each crucible into its own 250-mL erlenmeyer flask. Use deionized water from a wash bottle to effect complete transfer. If necessary, add additional water to each beaker until a total of about 50 mL is in the erlenmeyer flask. Adjust the mixtures to a pH of 1 by adding 6 M HCl and occasionally testing with a small piece of pH test paper. Heat the flasks on a steam bath or hot plate nearly to boiling for a total of about 20 minutes. If solid particles remain, filter by vacuum through Whatman #1 filter paper rinsing three times with hot deionized water. Transfer each filtrate *quantitatively* back to the 250-mL erlenmeyer flask by rinsing the suction flask several times with deionized water and adding the rinsings to the erlenmeyer flask.

Heat the contents of the erlenmeyer flasks to nearly boiling (if they are not already at that temperature) and add 15 mL of nearly boiling barium chloride solution fairly rapidly with vigorous stirring. Heat just under the boiling point for 1 hour. Filter the white barium sulfate precipitate in each erlenmeyer flask quantitatively by vacuum through a separate Whatman # 42 filter paper. Rinse any residual precipitate from the erlenmeyer flask to the filter paper with cold deionized water *at least* three times to achieve complete transfer of the precipitate and to thoroughly wash the precipitate.

Transfer the rinsed and drained filter papers and precipitates quantitatively back to the rinsed 250-mL erlenmeyer flasks, add (accurately with a buret) 35.00 mL 0.05 M EDTA solution and 5 mL 14 M aqueous ammonia. Boil gently for 15-20 minutes and add an additional 2 mL of aqueous ammonia about halfway through the boiling period to facilitate the dissolution of the precipitate. Allow the clear solution to cool (use an ice bath to hasten cooling), add 10 mL of pH=10 buffer solution, and add a few drops of EBT indicator. Titrate the unreacted EDTA in this solution to a wine-red with standard 0.05 M magnesium chloride solution.

A typical experiment gives the following results:

Concentration of EDTA solution = 0.0525 M
Concentration of $MgCl_2$ solution = 0.0500 M
Weight of coal sample = 1.0015 g
Titration of excess EDTA by $MgCl_2$ yields 26.45 mL

$$mol\ S = mol\ SO_4^{2-} = (0.03500\ L)(0.0500\ M)$$
$$- (0.02645\ L)(0.0525\ M) = 0.000361\ mol\ S$$

$$weight\ of\ sulfur\ = (32.06\ g/mol)(0.000361\ mol)$$
$$= 0.0116\ g$$

percent sulfur = $(0.01267\ g \div 1.0015\ g)(100) = 1.16\ \%$

For each of the three samples tested, determine the percent sulfur in the coal. Also, calculate the amount of sulfur burned and the amount of sulfur dioxide produced per hour by a power plant burning 600 tons of coal per hour.

Waste Disposal

All solutions may be rinsed down the drain with water.

Report the following Data:

Identity of Coal

Weight of Coal Samples

	1	2	3
crucible + contents	g	g	g
empty crucible	_____ g	_____ g	_____ g
weight of coal	g	g	g

Titration Results

	1	2	3
final buret reading	mL	mL	mL
initial buret reading	_____mL	_____mL	_____mL
volume of titrant	mL	mL	mL

Calculated Percent Sulfur in Coal

1.
2.
3.

Calculate the sulfur burned and the sulfur dioxide produced per hour by a power plant burning 600 tons of coal per hour.

1.
2.
3.

Discussion

Identify and **discuss** possible sources of error in this experiment which could lead to incorrect or inaccurate results. Whenever possible, indicate whether the experimental error being described would tend to cause high results, low results, or both high and low lack of precision.

Detection of Polycyclic Aromatic Hydrocarbons in Water

Polycyclic aromatic hydrocarbons (also known as polynuclear aromatic hydrocarbons or PAH) are organic molecules belonging to the family of compounds known as "aromatic hydrocarbons". They are formed by the combustion of carbon-containing fuels during processes such as forest fires, coal combustion, and the operation of gasoline and diesel engines, and even are found in cigarette smoke and charcoal-grill smoke. Many of the PAHs are known carcinogens. They are generally released into the atmosphere but eventually reach surface water. Some of the names and structures of PAHs are shown on the next page:

PAHs Studied in this Experiment

Common Name	Structure
Naphthalene	
Anthracene	
Phenanthrene	
Fluorene	
Chrycene	
Pyrene	
Acenaphthene	
Fluoranthene	

Low molecular weight PAHs, such as naphthalene, phenanthrene, and anthracene, tend to exist as vapors in the atmosphere. Higher molecular weight compounds, such as pyrene, exist as solids and are usually associated with soot particles. In general, the high molecular weight PAHs tend to be more carcinogenic than the smaller molecules.

Due to their nonpolar behavior, PAHs are hydrophobic and have very low water solubility. However, they are soluble at the part-per-million and part-per-billion level which is all that is necessary to make them a serious water pollution problem. In this experiment we use a solid-phase extraction cartridge (C18 Sep Pak or C18 Bond Elut) containing a nonpolar packing material to extract nonpolar PAH molecules from water. These nonpolar compounds are extracted from 500 mL of water and are rinsed (eluted) from the extraction cartridge with 2.0 mL of an organic solvent such as methanol or acetonitrile. The PAHs are thereby concentrated from an initial volume of 500 mL to a final volume of only 2.0 mL. The eluant, containing a much higher PAH concentration than the original water sample, is then analyzed by high-performance liquid chromatography.

Apparatus

A simple isocratic HPLC is all that is required for this determination. The recommended column is a Millipore/ Waters 25 cm stainless steel μBondapak C_{18} reverse-phase column. The mobile phase is a mixture of 50% H_2O and 50% CH_3CN (acetonitrile). A flow rate of about 1.5 mL/min usually works quite well. A spectrophotometric or filter-photometric detector set at a wavelength of 254 nm will yield excellent sensitivity. However, many PAHs absorb more strongly at shorter wavelengths such as 229 or 214 nm. Any of these wavelengths can be used with considerable success.

Procedure

Obtain eight 25-mL volumetric flasks for the preparation of solutions which will be used to establish the retention time of each PAH.

Flask 1: Pipet 5 mL of NAPHTHALENE stock (100 mg/L) solution into the flask and dilute to the mark with acetonitrile.

Flask 2: Pipet 5 mL of ANTHRACENE stock (100 mg/L) solution into the flask and dilute to the mark with acetonitrile.

Flask 3: Pipet 5 mL of PHENANTHRENE stock (100 mg/L) solution into the flask and dilute to the mark with acetonitrile.

Flask 4: Pipet 5 mL FLUORENE stock (100 mg/L) solution into the flask and dilute to the mark with acetonitrile.

Flask 5: Pipet 5 mL CHRYCENE stock (100 mg/L) solution into the flask and dilute to the mark with acetonitrile.

Flask 6: Pipet 5 mL PYRENE stock (100 mg/L) solution into the flask and dilute to the mark with acetonitrile.

Flask 7: Pipet 5 mL ACENAPHTHENE stock (100 mg/L) solution into the flask and dilute to the mark with acetonitrile.

Flask 8: Pipet 5 mL FLUORANTHENE stock (100 mg/L) solution into the flask and dilute to the mark with acetonitrile.

Obtain four 25 mL volumetric flasks for the preparation of standard mixtures.

Flask 1: Pipet 0.5 mL of EACH of the eight stock solutions into the flask and dilute to the mark with acetonitrile. (2.0 mg/L)

Flask 2: Pipet 1.0 mL of EACH of the eight stock solutions into the flask and dilute to the mark with acetonitrile. (4.0 mg/L)

Flask 3: Pipet 2.0 mL of EACH of the eight stock solutions into the flask and dilute to the mark with acetonitrile. (8.0 mg/L)

Flask 4: Pipet 2.5 mL of EACH of the eight stock solutions into the flask and dilute to the mark with acetonitrile. (10.0 mg/L)

Extraction and Trace Enrichment of PAH-Contaminated Water:

Prepare a "Contaminated" water sample by allowing a piece of creosote-treated wood weighing 25-50 grams to stand in about 3 liters of water with magnetic stirring for about a day. After this period of time, the water should take on a noticeable creosote odor.

Obtain 500 mL of the water sample. Also obtain a Sep Pak and pass 5 mL of acetonitrile through it with a glass syringe. Then rinse the Sep Pak with 5 mL water. Using a 30-mL syringe, run a 200-mL quantity of contaminated water through the Sep Pak. Organic contaminants are retained by the cartridge and the water may then be discarded. Deliver exactly 2.0 mL of acetonitrile through the Sep Pak and collect the 2.0 mL of acetonitrile in an autosampler vial for the high performance liquid chromatograph. All organic compounds are now in the acetonitrile 100 times more concentrated than in the original water sample.

In a similar fashion extract a 20-mL sample of water with a Sep Pak and again elute the contaminants from the Sep Pak with 2.0 mL of acetonitrile. Collect this 2.0-mL sample of acetonitrile in a vial for analysis by HPLC. This solution is 10 times as concentrated as the original water sample.

Chromatograph Separation

Place the vials in the autosampler tray and program the instrument so that each sample is identified in the sequence table. Start the automated sequence.

Waste Disposal

Dispose of standard solutions, all solvents, and extraction solutions in the organic waste container as directed by the instructor.

Analysis of Data

Determine the retention time of each of the eight PAHs and record each retention time on the report sheet. Then use the chromatograms of the four standard mixtures (2.0 mg/L, 4.0 mg/L, 8.0 mg/L, and 10.0 mg/L) to determine the peak area of each compound at each concentration. Record these values on the report sheet. Prepare a standard curve by plotting peak area (y-axis) for each of the eight compounds as a function of concentration in mg/L (on the x-axis). There will be eight lines on the graph -- one for each of the eight PAHs.

Of the peaks observed for the trace enriched water sample, decide which correspond to PAHs and identify those that were originally in the water. Calculate the concentration of each PAH in the enriched acetonitrile solution and in the contaminated water.

Report the Following Data:

Peak Areas and Retention times of Polycyclic Aromatic Hydrocarbons

Retention Times

_____ 1. Naphthalene
_____ 2. Anthracene
_____ 3. Phenanthrene
_____ 4. Fluorene
_____ 5. Chrycene
_____ 6. Pyrene
_____ 7. Acenaphthene
_____ 8. Fluoranthene

Peak Areas

1. 2.0 mg/L ___ 4.0 mg/L ___ 8.0 mg/L ___ 10.0 mg/L ___
2. 2.0 mg/L ___ 4.0 mg/L ___ 8.0 mg/L ___ 10.0 mg/L ___
3. 2.0 mg/L ___ 4.0 mg/L ___ 8.0 mg/L ___ 10.0 mg/L ___
4. 2.0 mg/L ___ 4.0 mg/L ___ 8.0 mg/L ___ 10.0 mg/L ___
5. 2.0 mg/L ___ 4.0 mg/L ___ 8.0 mg/L ___ 10.0 mg/L ___
6. 2.0 mg/L ___ 4.0 mg/L ___ 8.0 mg/L ___ 10.0 mg/L ___
7. 2.0 mg/L ___ 4.0 mg/L ___ 8.0 mg/L ___ 10.0 mg/L ___
8. 2.0 mg/L ___ 4.0 mg/L ___ 8.0 mg/L ___ 10.0 mg/L ___

Identity of PAH(s) detected in water

Retention Time	Compound	Peak Area
_____	1. _____	_____
_____	2. _____	_____
_____	3. _____	_____

Concentration(s) of PAH(s) detected in water

Compound	Concentration of Extracted Sample	Concentration in Water
1._____	_____	_____
2._____	_____	_____
3._____	_____	_____

Oxides of Sulfur, Carbon, Phosphorus, Nitrogen, Magnesium, and Calcium

General Discussion

The combustion of fossil fuels and the recovery of metals from ores containing their oxides or sulfides (smelting) leads to the formation of a variety of metal and nonmetal oxides. In many cases these oxides can have a significant impact on the environment--both detrimentally and beneficially.

Nonmetal oxides are *acid anhydrides* which means that they react with water to form acids. Environmentally important oxides are listed below:

Name	Formula	Rxn with Water	Name of Prod
Sulfur dioxide	SO_2	$SO_2 + H_2O \longrightarrow H_2SO_3$	Sulfurous acid
Sulfur trioxide	SO_3	$SO_3 + H_2O \longrightarrow H_2SO_4$	Sulfuric acid
Carbon monoxide	CO	none	None
Carbon dioxide	CO_2	$CO_2 + H_2O \longrightarrow H_2CO_3$	Carbonic acid
Nitric oxide	NO	None	None
Nitrogen dioxide	NO_2	$2NO_2 + H_2O \longrightarrow HNO_2 + HNO_3$	Nitrous acid Nitric
Phosphorus Pentoxide	P_2O_5	$P_2O_5 + 3H_2O \longrightarrow 2H_3PO_4$	Phosphoric aci
Magnesium oxide	MgO	$MgO + H_2O \longrightarrow Mg(OH)_2$	Magnesium hydro (Milk of magnes
Calcium oxide	CaO (Lime)	$CaO + H_2O \longrightarrow Ca(OH)_2$	Calcium hydroxi (Slaked lime)

The oxides of sulfur and nitrogen become acids which are responsible for "acid rain". Carbon dioxide causes even the purest rainwater to be somewhat acidic due to the formation of carbonic acid in precipitation. Conversely, magnesium hydroxide and calcium hydroxide are alkaline and can be used to neutralize acidity caused by nitrogen and sulfur oxides.

Apparatus

a. **Gas-collection bottles and square glass plates** for covering the bottles (4 per student group).
b. **Pneumatic trough** (1 for each group).
c. **Deflagrating spoon** (1 per group).
d. **Crucible and cover**.
e. **Plastic syringes.** 50- or 60-mL disposable syringes.

Reagents

a. **Potassium chlorate:** Solid, granular $KClO_3$.

b. **Manganese(IV) oxide:** Solid, powdered MnO_2

c. **Sulfur:** Solid powdered sulfur.

d. **Carbon:** Small lumps of charcoal.

e. **Copper:** Wire or mesh.

f. **Nitric acid (concentrated):** 15 M reagent grade HNO_3.

g. **Magnesium:** Turnings or ribbon.

h. **Calcium:** Granules or small pieces.

i. **Potassium permanganate solution:** 0.1 M $KMnO_4$ solution.

j. **Barium chloride solution:** 0.1 M $BaCl_2$ solution.

k. **pH test paper:** Wide range, pH 2-10.

l. **6 M HCl**

m. **6 M HNO_3**

n. **Phosphorus:** Amorphous red powder.

Procedure

Preparation of oxygen. Potassium chlorate decomposes when heated to produce oxygen gas and potassium chloride. The rate of decomposition even at 400-500 °C is too slow to produce useful amounts of oxygen unless a catalyst is added. Manganese(IV) oxide, also known as manganese dioxide, is a good catalyst.

Assemble the apparatus shown in Figure 1. The large test tube serves as the reaction vessel in which potassium chlorate is heated and oxygen is evolved. Make sure the rubber tubing, glass tubing, and stopper are in good condition and are connected to one another correctly. Use care if it is necessary to insert glass tubing into the stopper. Glass tubing breaks easily and can cause a bad cut.

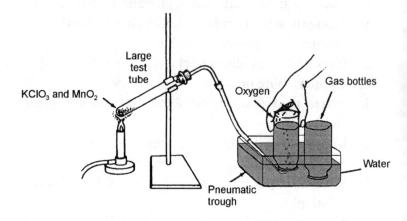

Figure 1. Apparatus for the generation of oxygen.

Fill a pneumatic trough about one-third to one-half full. Completely fill four gas collection bottles with water. Cover the first bottle with a glass plate, and transfer the bottle to the trough by inverting it and lowering it into the water with the glass still covering the mouth of the bottle. After the bottle is in the trough the glass can be removed and the bottle allowed to stand inverted in the trough. Repeat this procedure with the second bottle. The other two bottles can be put in the trough after the first two have been filled with oxygen and removed.

Weigh approximately 12 g of potassium chlorate ($KClO_3$) and 2 g of manganese(IV) oxide (MnO_2) in a small, dry beaker, mix them, and transfer them to the large test tube of the oxygen generator. The test tube should be tilted as shown in the diagram with the $KClO_3/MnO_2$ spread out so that its surface is parallel to the bench-top surface.

Connect the stopper securely to the test tube making sure that the potassium chlorate does not touch the stopper. Start heating the mixture in the test tube by gently applying heat with a Bunsen burner until the mixture begins to melt and oxygen begins to be evolved. **Note: potassium chlorate is a powerful oxidizing agent. Do not allow the molten material to contact the stopper or any combustible material because a fire may result.**

While one lab partner operates the burner, the other should move the gas outlet tube to the first bottle allowing bubbles of oxygen gas to fill the bottle and displace water from the bottle. Heat at a moderate intensity so that the each bottle fills in about a minute. As each bottle fills with oxygen, a glass plate should be slid over the mouth of the bottle while still under water. The bottle may then be removed and allowed to stand (mouth up) with the glass covering the bottle. When all four bottles are full, remove the gas outlet tube from the pneumatic trough and stop heating. Oxygen can be stored in these bottles for several hours because a reasonable gas-tight seal is produced by the small amount of water between the glass plate and the bottle mouth. After the mixture in the test tube has cooled, adding water to the test tube will partially dissolve the KCl and unreacted $KClO_3$ so that it can be poured out.

Oxidation of carbon. Using a Bunsen burner, clean out the cup of a deflagrating spoon by heating it strongly in the hottest part of the flame. After cooling, put into it a lump of charcoal about the size of a pea. Ignite it in a burner flame and immediately lower the spoon containing the glowing carbon into a bottle of oxygen by sliding the glass cover aside just enough to make room for it. Replace the cover as fully as possible while the reaction takes place (see Figure 2). When the oxidation reaction subsides, slip the cover aside, remove the deflagrating spoon, and add 5 mL of purified water. Replace the cover and shake to get carbon dioxide to dissolve in the water. Test the pH of the water with pH test paper. For comparison, test the pH of purified water with a separate strip of test paper.

Oxidation of sulfur. This procedure must be done in a fume hood. Clean the deflagrating spoon in a flame, allow to cool and put a small amount of sulfur (about 1/4 of its volume) into the spoon. Ignite the sulfur in a burner flame. Immediately lower the burning sulfur into an oxygen-filled bottle replacing the cover glass as fully as possible while the reaction proceeds. When the reaction subsides, remove the spoon and cover the bottle. Repeat this procedure a second time.

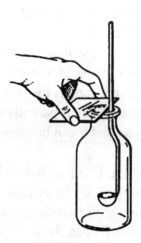

Figure 2. Combustion in a bottle of oxygen.

Add 5 mL of purified water to each bottle containing SO_x and shake with the cover in place to get the sulfur oxides to dissolve. Test the pH of the water. Transfer the water from each bottle to two separate test tubes.

To the first test tube, add one or two drops of 6 M nitric acid and a drop of potassium permanganate solution. Sulfite ion (from sulfurous acid) is a good reducing agent and will decolorize potassium permanganate. Sulfate ion (from sulfuric acid) will not. Is sulfite present? What gas was responsible for its formation?

To the second test tube, add 1 to 2 drops of barium chloride solution. The white precipitate is barium sulfate and/or barium sulfite. Add 1 mL of 6 N HCl. Barium sulfite is soluble in strongly acidic solution but barium sulfate remains undissolved. What can you conclude about the presence or absence of sulfate and sulfite? Which oxide or oxides of sulfur were formed?

Oxidation of phosphorus. This procedure must be done in a hood. Obtain a small amount of red phosphorus (about the size of a match head) and burn it in pure oxygen as was done for sulfur and carbon. Phosphorus is quite flammable so be careful! Allow the deflagrating spoon and phosphorus to remain in the bottle about 5 minutes until the burning completely stops. Add 5 mL of purified water and test the pII of the water containing dissolved phosphorus oxide.

Formation of nitrogen dioxide. Fortunately, the reaction between nitrogen gas and oxygen gas is not thermodynamically favored at room temperature. Yet combustion processes produce sufficiently high temperatures to cause nitrogen and oxygen to react to form nitric oxide. Nitric oxide readily reacts with oxygen to form nitrogen dioxide. In the laboratory, nitrogen dioxide is easily synthesized by allowing copper metal to react with concentrated nitric acid.

This procedure must be done in a hood. Place 0.1 gram of copper wire or mesh into a 250-mL erlenmeyer flask. Obtain one milliliter of concentrated nitric acid in a small beaker. With a dropper, add the acid dropwise until the gas is evolving fairly rapidly and the flask appears to be full of the colored gas. What color is NO_2?

Using a large plastic syringes with a short length of tubing connected to the tips, collect 40 mL of NO_2 into the syringe. Draw 5 mL of purified water into the syringe. Cap the syringe, shake well, and allow to stand for several minutes. Transfer the purified water to a beaker, and test its pH with test paper.

Oxidation of magnesium. Magnesium burns readily in the 21% oxygen concentration found in the air. Put a 2-cm strip of magnesium in a clean crucible. Strongly heat the crucible in a wire triangle on a ring stand using a Bunsen burner. **Note: Do not look at the burning magnesium because the intense light can damage the eyes.**

After the magnesium has reacted, transfer the magnesium oxide to a small test tube. Add one or two milliliters of water. Swirl to mix, and test the pH of the solution. How does it compare to the pH of purified water?

Oxidation of calcium. Repeat the same procedure with calcium that was used for magnesium using three or four granules of calcium in place of the magnesium ribbon. The calcium probably will not burn as the magnesium did, but it will oxidize if heated strongly in the flame. When most of the calcium appears to have oxidized, remove the heat, and allow the crucible to cool. Transfer the calcium oxide to a test tube; add water; and test the pH.

Waste Disposal

All solutions may be rinsed down the drain with water. Solids should be placed in a waste basket.

Data and Discussion

Record observations during evolution of oxygen (color of oxygen, rate of gas evolution, etc.).

Record pH of purified water and purified water with dissolved oxides including carbon dioxide, sulfur oxides, phosphorus oxide, nitrogen dioxide, magnesium oxide and calcium oxide. Which produce the most acidic and most basic solutions?

Answer question asked in various parts of the procedure. Record data in a logical order which reflects the order in which the experiment was carried out.

Finally, answer the following general questions:

1. What kinds of elements produce oxides which are acid anhydrides?

2. What kinds of elements produce oxides which are base anhydrides?

3. What might happen if a glowing splint fell into molten potassium chlorate?

4. From your observations in this experiment, what can you conclude about the degree of solubility of oxygen in water?

Sampling of NO_x $(NO + NO_2)$ and Particulates

(a modification of Ondrus, *J. Chem. Educ.*, **56** 1979, 551-552)

General Discussion

The oxides of nitrogen are receiving a great deal of attention as air pollutants. They are important because they participate in many photo-chemical reactions and are largely responsible for the formation of the "brown haze" of smog and the accompanying eye irritation and other physiological effects. Of the possible nitrogen oxides, only nitric oxide (NO) and nitrogen dioxide (NO_2), together referred to as NO_x, are of concern in air pollution studies.

NO is present in automobile exhaust in concentration ranging from a few parts per million (ppm or $\mu L/L$) to several thousand $\mu L/L$. Its toxicity is similar to that of carbon monoxide because it too combines strongly with hemoglobin in the blood. During the combustion of fossil fuels, nitrogen and oxygen in the air used combine at high temperature to form NO.

$$N_2 + O_2 \rightleftharpoons 2\,NO \qquad\qquad (I)$$

While most of the NO_x that is emitted in automobile exhaust is in the form of NO, nitrogen dioxide begins to form by the reaction on NO with excess oxygen.

$$2\,NO + O_2 \rightleftharpoons 2\,NO_2 \qquad\qquad (II)$$

NO_2 is a brown pungent gas. Concentrations of 20-50 µL/L NO_2 are irritable to the eyes. At only 150 µL/L there is danger of strong local irritations especially to the respiratory organs.

This experiment is based upon the fact that NO_2 dissolves in aqueous solutions to form nitrite ion. Nitrite reacts with sulfanilic acid and N-1-naphthylethylene-diamine in acetic acid to give an azo dye which can be analyzed spectrophotometrically.

Since the NO_2 reaction with water is:

$$2\,NO_2 + H_2O \rightleftharpoons 2\,H^+ + NO_2^- + NO_3^- \qquad\qquad (III)$$

the NO_2 to NO_2^- ratio is expected to be 2:1. However, chemists have determined experimentally that 1.39 mole of NO_2 produces the same color intensity as 1 mole of NO_2^- ion. This empirical observation is made use of in the final NO_x calculations.

Only NO_2 reacts with the color producing reagent. The gas being analyzed is allowed to stand undiluted in the presence of the indicator reagent until the reaction given by equation (II) has essentially occurred to completion. By doing this, the total NO_x concentration (NO + NO_2) is determined.

Because particulate matter would interfere with the colorimetric procedure described above, it is quantitatively filtered from the smoke or exhaust gas by means of a membrane filtration device. The number of milligrams of particulates on the filter is determined on an analytical balance by weighing the filter before and after it has been used.

Reagents

a. **Stock sodium nitrite solution**, 5.0 µg NO$_2^-$/mL. Dilute 1.50 g of NaNO$_2$ to 1.00 L. This solution contains 1000 µg NO$_2^-$ per mL. Then dilute the 1000 µg/mL NO$_2^-$ solution 200-fold, ie. 5.0 mL to 1000 mL.

b. **NO$_X$ indicator mixture**: Dissolve 5.0 g anhydrous sulfanilic acid in almost a liter of water containing 140 mL of glacial acetic acid. Add 0.20 g of N-1-naphthylethylenediamine hydrochloride and dilute to 1.00 L.

Apparatus

a. Five 60 cc plastic syringes
b. One 5 cc syringe
c. Cigarette holder - constructed from rubber or plastic tubing
d. Four membrane filters and one filter holder

Procedure

a. Sampling

Obtain four membrane filters, handling them only by the edge. Finger prints on the surface will greatly impair their filtering capacity. They should be handled gently to avoid poking holes in them or cracking them. Identify the filters by marking each with one or more dots on the edge using a felt tip pen. Weigh each filter separately on an analytical balance to the nearest 0.0001 g.

Place the first filter in the filter holder, and carefully connect the two holder halves tightening them snugly and being sure that the filter seats properly. Attach the membrane filter apparatus to an empty 60-mL syringe.

Rinse four other 60-mL syringes with a few milliliters of indicator reagent and then fill two with exactly 25 mL and two more with exactly 10 mL of the NO_x indicator. Make sure in each case that air bubbles have been expelled along with any excess solution. Cap the syringes and number them following the same scheme that was used for the filters. Carry out duplicate determinations using the following procedures on cigarette smoke and on automobile exhaust.

Cigarette Smoke

Connect the cigarette holder to the filter holder (see Figure 1). Light a cigarette making sure that the entire tip is smoldering. Immediately place it in the cigarette holder and use the empty 60-mL syringe to draw a 35-mL puff of two-seconds duration. Between puffs, the filter apparatus should be disconnected from the syringe to expel the filtered smoke into the air. Any visible cloudiness in the filtered smoke indicates that the millipore filter is either perforated or seated incorrectly. Wait one minute and draw a second 35-mL puff. After the second puff, the cigarette and filter holder should be transferred to the first indicator syringe containing 25 mL of reagent. When one minute has elapsed since the second puff, draw a 35-mL, two-second puff through the filter into the indicator syringe. This will necessitate pulling the plunger to the 60-mL mark.

Disconnect the filter holder from the syringe, cap the syringe, and shake vigorously. Allow the filtered smoke to remain in the syringe for at least 30 minutes with occasional shaking. The cigarette should be discarded and the membrane filter removed from its holder. When the color development is complete (at least 30 minutes) expel all gas from the syringe while retaining exposed indicator in the syringe. Draw 25 mL of unexposed indicator in the syringe. This dilution to a total of 50 mL is necessary to produce a color intensity which can be read with the spectrophotometer.

Repeat this procedure with a second cigarette.

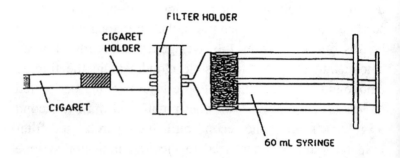

Figure 1. Apparatus for cigarette smoke analysis.

Automobile Exhaust

Replace the cigarette holder on the membrane filter holder with a short (3-4 inch) piece of rubber tubing (see Figure 2). Place the third filter in the holder and connect the holder to an empty syringe. Use the empty syringe to draw nine 50-mL aliquots of exhaust gas from an idling automobile through the filter. (The draw rate is not important in this case.) Transfer the filter holder to a syringe containing 10 mL of indicator reagent. Draw 50 mL of exhaust through the filter into the syringe by pulling the plunger to the 60-mL mark.

Disconnect the filter holder from the syringe, cap the syringe, and shake vigorously. Allow the filtered exhaust gas to remain in the syringe with the 10 mL of indicator for at least 30 minutes with occasional shaking.

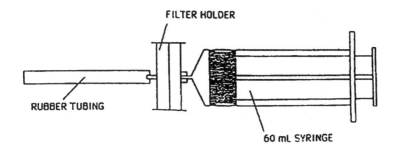

Figure 2. Apparatus for automobile exhaust analysis.

b. Standards (prepare using the 30 minute color development period)

1. Using a 5-mL syringe, add 1.00 mL of 5.0 µg/mL NO$_2^-$ solution to a 25-mL graduated cylinder. Dilute to the 25-mL mark with NO$_x$ indicator. Mix and pour 10-20 mL into a labeled test tube and stopper it securely. Discard the remaining solution and rinse the graduated cylinder with purified water.

2. Repeat the above procedure with 2.00 mL, 3.00 mL and 4.00 mL of stock nitrite solution. The concentrations of NO$_2^-$ represented by the four standard are 0.20 µg/mL, 0.40 µg/mL, 0.60 µg/mL, and 0.80 µg/mL, respectively. All four standard solutions should be kept in stoppered test tubes for 15 minutes or longer to ensure complete color development.

c. Data and Calculations

Reweigh all four membrane filters and determine the number of grams of particulate matter by subtraction. Convert grams of particulate matter to milligrams of particulate matter. Use equation (IV) to calculate the number of milligrams of particulate matter per cubic meter of sample.

$$mg / m^3 = \frac{mg \ particles}{total \ mL \ sampled} (1000 \ L / m^3) \qquad (IV)$$

With the spectrophotometer set to a wavelength of 550 nm, measure the absorbance of the four standards using unexposed NO_x indicator as a blank. Measure the absorbance of the four exposed indicator samples. Make a standard curve and use it to determine the concentration of nitrite ion (NO_2^-) in each exposed indicator solution.

Use equation (V) to calculate the number of micrograms of NO_x per liter.

$$mg \ NO_x/m^3 = \mu g \ NO_x/L = (\mu g \ NO_2^-/mL)(V_i/V_g)(1.39)(1000 \ mL/L) \quad (V)$$

where V_i is the total volume of indicator used, (50 mL for smoke, 10 mL for exhaust), V_g is the volume of gas sampled, (35 mL or 50 mL) and 1.39 is the factor for converting NO_2^- to NO_2.

Calculate the concentration in parts per million ($\mu L/L$) using equation (VI).

$$ppm \ NO_x = \mu L \ NO_x/L = [(\mu g \ NO_x/L)/46] \ [RT/P] \qquad (VI)$$

where R is the gas constant (0.082 L atm/°K mole), T is the absolute temperature (300°K), P is the pressure (1 atm), and 46 is the molecular weight of NO$_2$.

Finally, calculate the average μL/L concentration NO$_x$ for the cigarette and for the automobile exhaust.

Report the Following Data:
Cigarette brand: Automobile Make: Model: Year:

weight of filter in grams after sampling

weight of filter before sampling

grams of particulates

milligrams of particulates

volume (in mL) used for particulate sampling

concentration of particulates in mg/m^3

Average mg/m^3 for cigarette

Average mg/m^3 for automobile

Absorbance of Standards (Draw a Standard Curve)

0.20 µg NO_2^-/mL _____   0.60 µg NO_2^-/mL _____
0.40 µg NO_2^-/mL _____   0.80 µg NO_2^-/mL _____

	Cigarette		Automobile	
	1	2	3	4
Absorbance of exposed indicator sample				
NO_2^- concentration (µg/mL)				
Concentration of NO_x (mg/m^3)				
Average (mg/m^3)				
Concentration NO_x (µL/L)				
Average (µL/L)				

Preparation and Properties of Ozone

General Discussion

Ozone is an allotrope of oxygen having the molecular formula O_3. It is found in the stratosphere (12 - 15 miles above the Earth's surface) at concentrations up to 10 μL/L. In that region of the atmosphere, it plays the very important role of absorbing solar ultraviolet radiation that would otherwise reach the earth's surface. In particular, it absorbs UV-B radiation which is not readily absorbed by other molecular species in the atmosphere.

Ozone is also produced in the troposphere (essentially at ground level) as a pollutant during the formation of photochemical smog from chemicals found in industrial and car exhaust. Because it is a strong oxidizing agent, it is irritating to sensitive tissue such as the eyes, nasal passages, and the lungs. It can also be detrimental to plant foliar tissue, and it can accelerate the deterioration of metals, rubber, and plastic materials through a variety of oxidation mechanisms.

Ozone is formed in the stratosphere when ultraviolet light having a wavelength of 241 nm or shorter causes an oxygen (O_2) molecule to dissociate into two oxygen atoms (free radicals). The oxygen radicals then combine with other O_2 molecules to form ozone according to the following reaction mechanism:

$$O_2 + \text{a photon of UV light} \longrightarrow 2\,O\bullet$$
$$2\,O\bullet + 2\,O_2 \longrightarrow 2\,O_3$$

$$\text{Net Reaction:} \quad 3\,O_2 \xrightarrow{h\nu} 2\,O_3$$

Ozone is also converted back to diatomic oxygen (in the absence of catalysts such as chlorine radicals) through the interaction of UV radiation with the O_3 molecule. During the daylight hours, the rate of formation of ozone equals the rate of disappearance of ozone, and its concentration reaches a steady state.

The pungent odor of ozone is noticeable when the gas is formed by an electrical discharge. Ozone is a powerful oxidizing agent and an effective antiseptic and bleaching agent. In high concentrations it is a severe irritant.

This experiment is intended to allow the student to prepare ozone in the laboratory, measure its ultraviolet absorption spectrum, observe its ability to act as an oxidizing agent, and compare its oxidizing properties to other oxidizing agents.

Reagents

a. **0.1 M KI solution.** Dissolve 16.6 g of KI in enough water to prepare a liter of solution.

b. **Household bleach.**

c. **Chlorine water.** Prepare **in a hood** from household bleach (diluted 1 to 4) by slowly adding 6 N HCl until the mixture turns distinctly yellow. Prepare the chlorine water fresh just before lab and store in a glass stoppered bottle.

d. **3% hydrogen peroxide solution.**

e. **30% hydrogen peroxide solution.**

f. **FD&C food dyes.** Blue dye #1 and Red dye #40.

g. **Rubber bands.**

Apparatus

a. Distillation condenser with Tygon tubing on the water inlet and outlet (see Figure 1).
b. High-voltage (10,000 - 20,000 volts) coil.
c. Aluminum foil.
d. Scanning UV spectrophotometer with 2-cm and 5-cm cylindrical cells equipped with glass or Teflon stoppers.
e. Wooden frame with two glass tubes passing through one side of the frame and two glass plates to cover both faces of the frame (see Figure 2).
f. Spring clip made by cutting the ends from a wire test tube holder and retaining the handle portion of the holder (see Figure 2).

Procedure

a. Construction of ozone generator

Clamp a distillation condenser (make sure it is dry) to two ring stands as shown in Figure 1. Prepare a "tube" of aluminum foil about 12 inches long by forming the foil over a pencil or a dowel rod. This foil tube must be inserted through the center of the condenser and should run through most of the length of the condenser. Leave enough of the foil tube exposed so that a wire from the high-voltage coil can be connected to it by means of an alligator clip.

Wrap a layer or two of foil over the outer condenser jacket leaving a tab of foil to which the other wire from the coil may be connected by means of another alligator clip. Hold the foil in place with cellophane tape. Keep the foil away from the metal of the ring stand. One flexible (Tygon) tube, connected to the condenser jacket, should run to a low-pressure air source and the other tube should have a Pasteur pipet with a fairly long thin tip connected to it.

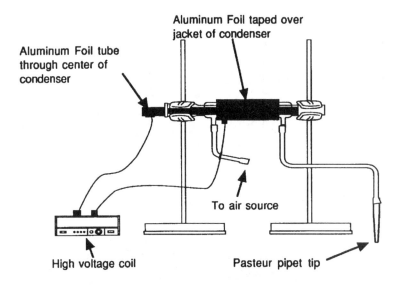

Figure 1. Apparatus for generation of ozone.

Open the air valve to which the hose from the condenser is connected, and carefully and use the valve to adjust the flow of air through the condenser. The flow rate should be such that if the tip of the Pasteur pipet is put in water, a gentle stream of bubbles issues from the tip of the pipet.

Oxidizing Properties of Ozone

Once the flow of air has been adjusted through the ozone generator, direct the flow from the generator through a cell constructed from a wooden frame covered with two pieces of glass held in place with rubber bands. Inside the cell put a wire spring with a rubber band stretched over its ends as shown in Figure 2. The wire spring is made from a test tube holder by clipping the ends of the holder and keeping the spring handle.

175

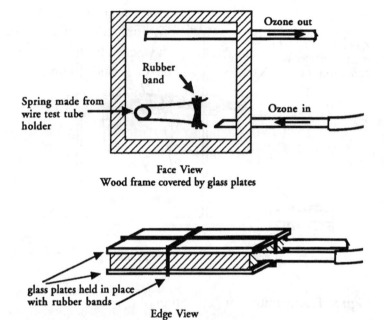

Face View
Wood frame covered by glass plates

Edge View

Figure 2. Cell for testing the effect of ozone on a stretched rubber band.

Connect one wire from the high voltage coil to the aluminum foil on the inside of the generator, and connect the other wire to the foil on the outside. Make sure no one is touching the apparatus. Turn on the coil. If there is any arcing between parts of the generator, turn off the power, remove the wires, and adjust the unit so that metal surfaces are farther apart to reduce arcing.

While the generator is operating, note whether the pungent odor of ozone can be detected. Do not intentionally try to detect the odor of ozone. It will probably be noticed during the course of the experiment. Allow the ozone from the generator to flow over the rubber band for a minute or two. **To minimize exposure to ozone, the instructor may request that students set up the apparatus in a hood.** Then turn off the electricity to the generator, remove the rubber band and spring from the cell, and compare the ozone-treated rubber band with an "untreated" one.

Compare the oxidizing power of ozone to chlorine, sodium hypochlorite, and hydrogen peroxide by the following tests:

1. 0.1 N KI. Put 5 mL of KI solution into five separate test tubes. With the electricity to the ozone generator turned off, place the Pasteur tip from the generator into the first tube so that air from the ozone generator bubbles through the KI. With hands well away from the apparatus, turn on the power and note whether a chemical change occurs in the tube in a minute or two. Oxidizing agents cause iodide to be oxidized to iodine which produces a yellow color. As more iodine is formed in solution, the solution becomes brown in color. Does ozone cause iodide to be oxidized to iodine?

To the second tube, add a few drops of chlorine water, and note any change in the iodide solution. To the third add household bleach (sodium hypochlorite solution) and look for a color change. To the fourth add a few drops of 3% hydrogen peroxide, and to the last tube add a few drops of 30% hydrogen peroxide. If no significant color change occurs, try adding a little more of the oxidizing agent.

Strong oxidizing agents cause iodide ion to be oxidized to iodine. The solution turns yellow or brown as the reaction happens. Record information about the apparent relative oxidizing power of the various oxidants tested. How does ozone compare to the other oxidizing agents in terms of reactivity with iodide?

2.   Food coloring. Add a few drops of FD&C red dye to about 100 mL of water in a beaker. Test the oxidizing power of ozone and the other oxidizing agents using five separate 5-mL samples of the colored solution as was done with KI above.

Run the same tests using blue food coloring. Again record observations along with similarities and differences between the oxidizing agents. Which of the oxidizing agents are most effective in bleaching the color of food colorings?

Ultraviolet Spectrum of Ozone

Use a dry cylindrical 2-cm spectrophotometer cell with quartz windows and containing only air to run a "blank" or base-line spectrum on the scanning spectrophotometer. Scanning from 200 nm to 400 nm is appropriate, but the entire visible and UV range from 200 to 800 may be scanned.

If the Pasteur tip from the ozone generator is wet, either dry it or replace it with a dry one. Put the end of the tip into the opening of the cell as far in as it will go. Turn on the power and allow ozone-containing air to pass into and out of the cell for a minute or two. Turn off the power to the generator, remove the Pasteur tip, and immediately cap the cell. Measure the absorption spectrum of the gas within the cell as soon as possible. Prepare a "hard copy" of the spectrum and note the absorption maximum (λ_{max})as well as the wavelength range of UV absorption.

If time permits, perform a similar measurement using a 5-cm cell and using two 5-cm cells in series. This should provide information on the effect of path length on the maximum absorbance reading. Is the wavelength range or the wavelength of maximum absorbance (λ_{max}) affected by changing the path length?

What UV regions (UV-A, UV-B, or UV-C) are absorbed most strongly and most completely by ozone. Why would a wide ozone band be better than a narrow one in the stratosphere?

Gas-Phase Analysis of Air Components and Air Pollutants Using Fourier-Transform Infrared Spectrophotometry

(a modification of Amey, *J. Chem. Educ.*, **5** (69) 1992, A148-A151)

General Discussion

Like the UV-Vis photodiode array spectrophotometer, the Fourier-transform infrared spectrophotometer is a computer-driven rapid scanning instrument which allows students to gather a great deal of data in a relatively short period of time. Environmentally important molecules, including nitrogen oxides, carbon monoxide, carbon dioxide, hydrocarbons, water vapor, and chlorofluorocarbons, all absorb infrared radiation at specific wavelengths. This is useful in the identification of these compounds in samples of air and other gas-phase mixtures. The fact that these compounds absorb IR radiation, in some cases fairly strongly, explains why several are considered to be "greenhouse" gases which may contribute to the greenhouse effect and global warming.

In this experiment, we use plastic syringes and balloons to collect gas samples and to qualitatively analyze for important air components and air pollutants. Balloons are filled to a predetermined size with the gas or gas mixture to be tested. Then the balloon is placed in the path of the infrared beam of the FTIR. The beam passes through the rubber film of the balloon with IR radiation being absorbed both by the rubber and by the gases inside the balloon. The absorption spectrum of the balloon contributes to the background spectrum which is obtained when a balloon filled with nitrogen (which is infrared transparent) is placed in the sample compartment. The computer data system allows the background spectrum to be subtracted from spectra obtained using balloons containing other gases.

Note

To allow students maximum instrument time, this experiment may be performed simultaneously with experiment 18. Half of the students would do one experiment and half would do the other.

Materials

a. Uninflated rubber balloons of 2.5-in. diameter uninflated.
b. Rubber tubing
c. 4-in. and 3-in. i.d. lab-type iron rings.
d. Plastic disposable syringes, 60-mL.
e. Syringe needles, 22 gauge.

Instrumentation

Fourier-transform infrared spectrophotometer (FTIR) capable of rapid, repeated scanning and equipped with a computer data system which will subtract background spectra and produce hard copies of spectra with a printer or a plotter.

Procedure

Stretch the nozzle of a balloon over the open end of a piece of rubber or plastic tubing connected to the regulator on a nitrogen compressed-gas cylinder. Carefully open the valve on the outlet end of the regulator and inflate the balloon with nitrogen. The balloon may be inflated to slightly over 10 centimeters (4 inches) and the excess gas allowed to escape during the process of adjusting the diameter of the balloon . Before tying a knot in the balloon nozzle, nitrogen should be allowed to escape until the balloon is just 4 inches in diameter. It should just fit inside a 4-inch laboratory ring. A total of five balloons prepared in this manner will be required. Place the balloon on the holder (an evaporating dish serves as a good holder) in the IR spectrophotometer cell compartment. Run a spectral scan on the N_2-filled balloon as a "background" spectrum. It may be helpful to mark the side of the balloon so that it can later be placed in the cell compartment in about the same orientation.

Generation of a gas. When generating a gas, a small (250-mL) vacuum flask should be used. A stopper should be placed in the mouth of the flask and a 6-inch piece of tubing attached to the side arm. The gas should be allowed to vent through the tubing. After a needle (22 gauge, attached to a 60-mL plastic syringe) is inserted through the side of the tube, the tubing should be closed with a pinch clamp. The internal pressure will fill the syringe with the gas being generated. It may be necessary to pull the plunger gently to aid in the filling of the syringe. When the needle is removed from the tubing, the pinch clamp should be released. The gas in the syringe may be introduced into a balloon as outlined later. Syringe tips may be covered with Parafilm® if the gas is to remain in the syringes for a while.

1. **Dry CO_2.** Put several pieces of dry ice into the flask. Sublimation will quickly result in adequate CO_2 generation. Fill one 60-mL syringe for later introduction into a balloon already filled with "dry-nitrogen".

2. **Wet CO_2.** Cover the bottom of the flask with about 1/2 inch of hot water. Add two Alka-Seltzer tablets and replace the stopper. Effervescence will result in adequate CO_2 generation along with a significant water vapor content. Fill two 60-mL syringes for later introduction into a balloon already filled with "dry-nitrogen".

3. **Water vapor.** Replace the solid stopper in the vacuum flask with a one-hole stopper containing a piece of glass tubing that will reach nearly to the bottom of the flask. Fill the flask half-full with water that has recently been boiling. Replace the stopper. Connect the glass tube to the hose from the nitrogen tank and bubble nitrogen through the hot water. The "wet" nitrogen coming out the side arm should be used to fill two 60-mL syringes

for later introduction into a balloon already filled with "dry-nitrogen".

Compressed carbon monoxide. In a similar fashion, syringes can be filled with carbon monoxide from a small cylinder (**in a hood!**) by attaching a 6-inch piece of rubber tubing to the gas-regulator outlet. The tubing should be clamped with a pinch clamp and about 5 psi pressure adjusted with the low-pressure stage of the regulator. The syringe should be equipped with a 22-gauge needle. Once the needle is inserted through the pressurized rubber tubing, the syringe will easily fill with very little gas waste or loss to the air. Caution, if the gas pressure is set too high, the syringe may fill too rapidly shooting the plunger out of the syringe. This will do little harm but may startle the student. Fill two 60-mL syringes for later introduction into a balloon already filled with "dry-nitrogen".

Cigarette smoke or exhaust samples. Cigarette smoke should be drawn directly into a 60-mL plastic syringe by sliding one end of the cigarette into a short piece of flexible tubing of the correct inside diameter (about 3/8 in) to hold the cigarette snugly and connecting the other end of the tubing to the Luer collar on the syringe. A 60-mL sample of smoke may be drawn directly into the syringe. Automobile exhaust gas should be sampled with a longer (8-inch) piece of tubing attached to a 60-mL syringe. The open end of the tubing is used to draw exhaust from the tail pipe of a vehicle which has been allowed to run for several minutes prior to sampling. Fill five 60-mL syringes with **either** cigarette smoke or automobile exhaust gas for later introduction into a balloon already filled with "dry-nitrogen".

Introducing samples into balloons. Once a gas has been collected in a 60-mL syringe, it should be introduced into a sealed nitrogen-filled balloon immediately after the background spectrum on that balloon has been run. Attach a 22-gauge needle to the Luer fitting of the syringe and carefully insert the needle through the thick rubber part of the balloon right next to the knot tied in the nozzle. The balloon will not break (usually) and the needle hole will seal when the needle is removed. The contents of 5 or more syringes may be introduced into the balloon in this manner. The needle may be removed and reinserted many times with no problem. Each balloon should be used for only one sample and then discarded.

Data

The plotter, connected to the spectrophotometer, should be used to produce "hard copies" of the following spectra:

1. A base-line obtained by running a "sample" scan right after the "background" scan.
2. Dry CO_2.
3. Wet CO_2.
4. Water vapor.
5. Carbon monoxide.
6. Either cigarette smoke or automobile exhaust.
7. Human breath. (Fill a balloon with nitrogen to the 4-inch size and pinch, but do not tie, the nozzle. Run a background spectrum. Then immediately release the N_2 from the balloon and reinflate to the 4-inch size by blowing up the balloon with your breath. Tie the nozzle and run a "sample" scan.)

Report the Following Data:

Wavelength(s) used to identify each gas

1. CO_2 _____ _____ _____ _____
2. H_2O _____ _____ _____ _____
3. C O _____ _____ _____ _____

Gases identified in mixtures (In each case explain how you identified each gas)

1. Wet CO_2 _____
_____
_____

   Explanation:

2. Cigarette Smoke _____
_____
_____

   Explanation:

3. Automobile _____
_____
_____

   Explanation:

4. Breath _____
_____
_____

   Explanation:

Exponential Decay of a Transition Metal Complex Ion

Iron (II) ion, Fe^{++} combines with the chelating ligand, 1,10-phenanthroline, to form the complex ion tris (1,10-phenanthroline) iron (II). An equation for the reaction forming this complex is given below. Note that 1,10-phenanthroline is abbreviated as "phen".

$$Fe^{++} + 3 \text{ phen} \longrightarrow Fe\,(phen)_3^{++} \qquad (I)$$

However, this complex ion is unstable in the presence of acids (pH < 3) and decomposes according to the reverse of equation I following first-order exponential decay.

$$Fe\,(phen)_3^{++} \longrightarrow Fe^{++} + 3 \text{ phen} \qquad (II)$$

This experiment is designed to demonstrate the effect of temperature on the rate of a chemical decay process. It allows the student to plot exponential data and to calculate the half life of an exponential change.
The equation for exponential decay is

$$-d[Fe\,(phen)_3^{++}]/dt = k[Fe\,(phen)_3{++}] \qquad (III)$$

The integrated form of this equation is

$$\ln [Fe (phen)3++] = -kt + \ln [Fe (phen)3++]_o \qquad (IV)$$

and the half life is calculated

$$t_{1/2} = .693/k \qquad (V)$$

Reagents

a. **1,10-phenanthroline solution**: Dissolve 1.0 g of 1,10-phenanthroline in about 800 mL of purified water at about 80 °C. Cool and dilute to 1000 mL.

b. **Iron (II) solution, 1000 mg/L**: Dissolve 3.512 g of ferrous ammonium sulfate in about one hundred milliliters of purified water. Add two drops of concentrated hydrochloric acid, and dilute to 500 mL.

c. **3 M sulfuric acid**:

Experimental Procedure

With a pipet, measure 10 mL of 1000 mg/L iron (II) solution into a 1000-mL volumetric flask and dilute to 1.0 liter with purified water. This solution contains 10 mg/L iron. With a graduated cylinder, measure 100 mL of the 10 mg/L iron (II) solution, and transfer to a 250-mL beaker. Also, with the graduated cylinder, measure 100 mL of 1,10-phenanthroline solution, and add this to the iron (II) solution in the beaker. Label this "solution A". What is the concentration of complexed iron in this solution (in mg/L Fe)? This solution will serve as the starting solution for decomposition experiments, and it will be used as a standard and to prepare other more dilute standards.

Have a Spectronic 20 (or 21) set up and ready to make absorbance measurements at a wavelength of 510 nm. Use two cuvettes. One should be kept full of purified water for zeroing the instrument, and the other should be used to measure absorbances.

Obtain three 125-mL erlenmeyer flasks. Place one in a warm water bath at 45 °C; place the second in a water bath at 35 °C; and keep the third flask at just above room temperature (25 °C). Put 50 mL of the iron phenanthroline solution into each of the three flasks. Then add 10 mL of 3 M sulfuric acid solution (which should be equilibrated at the same temperature as the solution in the 50-mL flask). The decomposition reaction now begins! Immediately measure the absorbance of a small portion (use a pipet to remove 4 mL from the flask) of the 45 °C mixture, and then either discard the small amount used or return it to the flask from which it was taken (the instructor will recommend what to do). Do the same thing with the other two solutions at the other two temperatures. Record the three absorbances as the 0 time readings. Every five minutes for one hour, absorbance readings for each of the three mixtures should be measured. Discard the liquid used for absorbance readings because its temperature is likely to change while taking the reading, and this might change the temperature in the reaction flask.

While the reaction kinetics are being measured, one of the two people working together on this experiment should prepare three more standards by diluting 15 mL, 10 mL, and 5 mL of "solution A" to a total of 20 mL in each case with a graduated cylinder. Calculate the complexed-iron concentrations in these three standards and record.

Plots

1. When all data has been recorded, use the standards and their absorbances to prepare a standard curve. Then use the standard curve to determine the iron concentration for each absorbance measured during the decomposition runs.

2. On a second piece of graph paper plot iron concentration (y-axis) for each decomposition experiment as a function of time (x-axis). Draw a smooth curve through each set of data points.

3. On a third piece of graph paper, plot for each decomposition experiment, the natural log of iron concentration (y-axis) as a function of time. Use a ruler to draw a straight line through the points for each experiment. From equation V it can be seen that the slope of each of the log plots is equal to -k for that reaction. Thus, calculate and record the slope of each of the lines and record on the report sheet.

Final Calculations

Using the slopes of the three lines on plot 3, calculate the half life of each of the three reactions. Remember to use significant figure rules discussed earlier. How is the rate of decay of a transition metal complex ion affected by temperature? Compare to the effect that moderate temperature changes are believed to have on the rate of decay of radioisotopes.

Report the Following Data:

Standards

Concentration Fe   Absorbance

_____   _____

_____   _____

_____   _____

_____   _____

Decomposition Runs

Time(min)	Abs	Fe concn	Ln [Fe]	
0	____	_____	_____	
5	____	_____	_____	
10	____	_____	_____	
15	____	_____	_____	
20	____	_____	_____	
25	____	_____	_____	Run 1 (25 °C)
30	____	_____	_____	
35	____	_____	_____	
40	____	_____	_____	
45	____	_____	_____	
50	____	_____	_____	
55	____	_____	_____	
60	____	_____	_____	

Time(min)	Abs	Fe concn	Ln [Fe]	
0	___	___	___	
5	___	___	___	
10	___	___	___	
15	___	___	___	
20	___	___	___	
25	___	___	___	Run 1 (35 °C)
30	___	___	___	
35	___	___	___	
40	___	___	___	
45	___	___	___	
50	___	___	___	
55	___	___	___	
60	___	___	___	

Time(min)	Abs	Fe concn	Ln [Fe]	
0	___	___	___	
5	___	___	___	
10	___	___	___	
15	___	___	___	
20	___	___	___	
25	___	___	___	Run 1 (45 °C)
30	___	___	___	
35	___	___	___	
40	___	___	___	
45	___	___	___	
50	___	___	___	
55	___	___	___	
60	___	___	___	

Calculated results

	Run 1 (45°)	Run 2 (35°)	Run 3 (25°)
slope = of Ln [Fe] vs. time plots	_____	_____	_____
value of k =	_____	_____	_____
Half life =	_____	_____	_____

Include correct units and correct significant figures in the above calculated results.

How is half life affected by temperature and how does this contrast with the effect of temperature on nuclear decay reactions?

Single-Digestion Procedure for Determining Phosphorus, Calcium, Magnesium, Potassium, and Nitrogen in Plant Tissue

General Discussion

This procedure was developed for the relatively rapid determination of a variety of important nutrients in environmental foliar tissue. It has been used for research projects involving replicate determination of a large number of samples. Many parts of the procedure can be hastened by using mechanical pipets and mechanical fluid delivery systems for reagents. The instructor may chose to have students do only part of the procedure. The procedure has been used by the author or by student researchers for analysis of animal feed, bog plants and peat, and lake algae. It has been tested against standard reference materials with certified values and has proven to produce remarkably reproducible and accurate results.

The digestion involves hot sulfuric acid and is potentially dangerous. It should be carried out in a fume hood. The student should wear adequate eye protection and clothing protection because even cold sulfuric acid will quickly damage most organic matter which it contacts.

The range of standards suggested for the metal ions may not always be quite correct for the plant tissue chosen to be tested. The standards can be adjusted or the dilution factor changed by the instructor or by the perceptive student.

Initial rinsing of glassware with dilute hydrochloric or sulfuric acid is a good idea (particularly to remove traces of phosphorus). After that, good lab technique and rinsing with deionized water is generally sufficient to produce great results.

Reagents for Phosphorus Determination

a. **Vanadomolybdate reagent**: Solution #1: Weigh 12.5 g ammonium molybdate and dissolve in 200 mL water. Dilute to 2.0 L.
Solution #2: Weigh 0.625 g of ammonium meta-vanadate (NH_4VO_3) and dissolve in 150 mL boiling water. Cool, add 10 mL con H_2SO_4 to the vanadate solution. Dilute to 2.0 L.
Mix equal volumes of solutions #1 and #2 just prior to use.

b. **50 mg/L phosphate (phosphorus) stock solution**: Dissolve 219.5 mg (0.2195 g) anhydrous potassium dihydrogen phosphate (KH_2PO_4) in purified water and dilute to 1.0 L.

Calcium, Magnesium, and Potassium Stock Solutions

c. **500 mg/L calcium stock solution**: To 1.249 g of oven-dried primary standard $CaCO_3$, add 50 mL purified water. Add dropwise a minimum volume of HCl ($\approx$ 10 mL) to completely dissolve the solid. Dilute to 1.0 L with purified water.

d. **500 mg/L magnesium stock solution**: Place 0.500 g magnesium metal (analytical reagent grade) in 50 mL purified water. Slowly add 10 mL con HCl to take the metal into solution as aqueous magnesium chloride. Dilute to 1.0 L with purified water.

e. **1000 mg/L potassium stock solution**: Dissolve 1.907 g of oven-dried analytical reagent grade KCl in purified water and dilute to 1.0 L.

Digestion Reagents

f. **Concentrated sulfuric acid**: Reagent grade.

g. **Na_2SO_4-$CuSO_4$ Digestion Mixture**: Mix thoroughly 100 g of powdered anhydrous Na_2SO_4 and 1.5 g powdered anhydrous $CuSO_4$. Be sure that all lumps of Na_2SO_4 are broken up.

Kjeldahl Distillation and Titration Reagents

h. **Methyl red indicator**: Dissolve 0.02 g in 60 mL ethanol and dilute to 100 mL with water.

i. **Bromcresol green indicator**: Dissolve 0.1 g bromcresol green in 100 mL ethanol or dissolve 0.1 g bromcresol green sodium salt in 100 mL water.

j. **4% Boric acid/mixed indicator mixture**: Dissolve 40 g boric acid in 900 mL purified water. Add 10 mL methyl red indicator and 10 mL bromcresol green indicator. Dilute to 1000 mL with water.

k. **Sodium carbonate solution (Na_2CO_3), 0.10 N:** Primary standard grade Na_2CO_3 should be dried for 4 hours at 250 °C and allowed to cool in a desiccator. Weigh, in a small beaker, about 0.53 g to the nearest 0.1 milligram and transfer quantitatively to a 100-mL volumetric flask by rinsing with purified or deionized water through a funnel into the flask. Dilute to the mark with purified or deionized water. The equivalent weight of Na_2CO_3 is 53.00. Calculate the exact normality of the Na_2CO_3 solution based on the weight diluted in the flask.

l. **Standard hydrochloric acid titrant, 0.10 N:** Transfer 8.3 mL of concentrated (12 N) reagent-grade HCl to a 1000-mL volumetric flask and dilute to the mark with purified or deionized water. This solution has a concentration of about 0.1 N.

Standardize by pipetting 25.00 mL of 0.10 N Na_2CO_3 solution into a 250-mL erlenmeyer flask and diluting to about 100 mL with purified or deionized water. Titrate using a bromcresol green/methyl red mixture (use 10 drops of each indicator) until a color change from blue to red appears. Titrate to an intermediate color between blue and red. Determine the normality of the HCl using the equation: (mL HCl) × (N HCl) = (mL Na_2CO_3) × (N Na_2CO_3)

m. Concentrated NaOH solution, 50% NaOH: Mix equal weights of purified water and solid NaOH pellets. To prepare a little over 100 mL of this solution, mix 100 mL of water (about 100 g of water) and 100 g of NaOH. This is a very concentrated NaOH solution, so be careful. The solution becomes very hot while the NaOH is dissolving. *It must be allowed to cool before using it for the Kjeldahl distillation.*

n. Mossy zinc: About 3 or 4 pieces, 1 to 2 g total, are required for each distillation.

Experimental Procedure

Weigh precisely 0.50 g dry powdered tissue in a digestion tube (usually a 100-mL or 250-mL Kjeldahl digestion flask). Add 4 g Na_2SO_4-$CuSO_4$ mixture and 10 mL con H_2SO_4. Digest until a clear, green-colored solution is produced (about an hour). Cool.

Upon cooling, the green color will fade to a nearly colorless to pale blue solution, and the salts in the mixture may crystallize to a nearly solid mass. Use purified water to quantitatively transfer the contents of the digestion flask to a 100-mL volumetric flask. Allow to cool before diluting the mixture in the volumetric flask to the 100-mL mark.

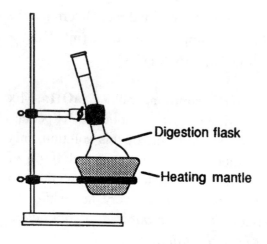

Digestion setup

Blank and Standards

o. **Blank:** Add 4 g of the Na_2SO_4-$CuSO_4$ mixture and 8.0 mL con H_2SO_4 to about 50 mL H_2O in a 100-mL volumetric flask. Swirl to dissolve. After cooling to room temperature, dilute to 100 mL with purified water.

p. **Standards, 10 and 20 mg/L phosphorus:** Transfer 20.0 mL and 40.0 mL of the 50.0 mg/L phosphorus stock solution to separate 100-mL volumetric flasks. Add purified water to bring the volume in each flask up to about 50 mL. Add 4 g of the Na_2SO_4-$CuSO_4$ mixture and 8.0 mL con H_2SO_4 to each flask. (Note: 8.0 mL H_2SO_4 is used rather than 10 mL because this is close to the amount expected to remain in a digestion flask after digestion is completed. The color development with vanadomolybdate reagent seems to be somewhat acid dependent.) Swirl to dissolve. After cooling to room temperature, dilute to 100 mL with purified water.

q. **Standards - 5.0 mg/L Mg, 25.0 mg/L Ca, 50.0 mg/L K:** Transfer 1.0 mL of stock 500 mg/L Mg solution, 5.0 mL of stock 500 mg/L Ca solution, and 5.0 mL of stock 1000 mg/L K solution to a 100 mL volumetric flask. Add purified water to bring the volume up to about 50 mL. Add 4 g of the Na_2SO_4-$CuSO_4$ mixture and 10.0 mL con H_2SO_4. Swirl to dissolve. After cooling to room temperature, dilute to 100 mL with purified water.

r. **Standards - 10.0 mg/L Mg, 50.0 mg/L Ca, 100.0 mg/L K:**
Repeat the directions in part **m** above using 2.0, 10.0, and 10.0 mL, respectively, of the Mg, Ca, and K stock solutions.

s. **Standards - 20.0 mg/L Mg, 100.0 mg/L Ca, 200.0 mg/L K:**
Repeat the directions in part **m** above using 4.0, 20.0, and 20.0 mL, respectively, of the Mg, Ca, and K stock solutions.

Procedure for Phosphorus Determination

Transfer to separate 50-mL beakers or flasks 5.0-mL portions of blank, standard and each digest. To each add a 20.0-mL aliquot of vanadomolybdate reagent with swirling to mix. A yellow color, which is stable for hours, develops in less than 5 minutes.

Use a spectrophotometer to measure the absorbance of each standard and each sample by pouring each solution in a cuvette and measuring its absorbance at 400 nm. A portion of the blank solution in a cuvette should be used to set 0.000 absorbance.

Prepare a standard curve by plotting absorbance as a function of concentration. Using the absorbance of each digested sample, determine the concentration of phosphorus in that digest from the standard curve. Calculate percent phosphorus using the equation below:

$$\% \, P = \left(\frac{(\text{mg Phosphorus} / \text{L})(0.100 \, \text{L})}{(\text{g sample})} \right)\left(\frac{1 \, \text{g}}{1000 \, \text{mg}} \right)(100)$$

Procedure for Ca, Mg, and K Determination

Dilute the blank, standards, and each digested sample 25-fold (1.00 mL to 25.00 mL) in volumetric flasks. Put the magnesium lamp in the lamp holder, and set the atomic absorption spectrophotometer to the appropriate wavelength, slit, lamp current, and photo-multiplier voltage as recommended for magnesium in the instrument manual. Since the analytical wavelength for magnesium is below 300 nm, background correction for magnesium is recommended if a background corrector is available on the instrument.

Aspirate the 25-fold diluted blank, and use it to zero the instrument. After the instrument has been zeroed, measure the absorbances of the 25-fold diluted standards and digests.

Repeat the determination using the calcium and potassium lamps. Background correction is not necessary for these elements.

Standard curves for each of the three metal ions should be prepared by plotting their absorbance as a function of their concentration. With the aid of the standard curve, determine the concentration of the metal ion using the absorbance of each 25-fold diluted digested sample. Calculate percent by weight in the undigested tissue using in the equation below:

$$\% \text{ metal} = \left(\frac{(\text{mg metal} / \text{L})(0.100 \text{ L})}{(\text{g sample})}\right)\left(\frac{25 \text{ g}}{1 \text{ mg}}\right)\left(\frac{1 \text{ g}}{1000 \text{ mg}}\right)(100)$$

Procedure for Kjeldahl Distillation and N Determination

After the digested samples have been diluted and used for phosphorus and metal ion analysis, the remaining solution (which should be 90 mL or more) may be used to determine percent nitrogen. Use a graduated cylinder to measure (as accurately as possible) 90 mL of the digested (and diluted) tissue sample or of the blank to a 250-mL round-bottom boiling flask like that shown in the diagram below. Volumes other than 90 mL may be used depending on how much of the solution is left after P, K, Ca, and Mg analysis.

Use a graduated cylinder to measure about 25 mL 50% NaOH. This solution is carefully poured down the inside of the boiling flask so as to form two layers (NaOH on bottom). Several "chunks" of mossy zinc must then be added as a boiling aid to the flask. Place a 250-mL erlenmeyer flask, containing 50 mL of 4% boric acid with methyl red/bromcresol green indicator, under the condenser with the outlet tube of the condenser just below the surface of the boric acid solution.

Mix the contents of the boiling flask by swirling. *NOTE: This is very important. The NaOH solution and the digestion mixture must be mixed before heat is applied.* Put the flask in the heating mantle, and connect the flask to the distillation adapter and condenser. Apply heat to begin the distillation. Continue the distillation for about 30-45 minutes until the total volume in the erlenmeyer flask is about 100 mL.

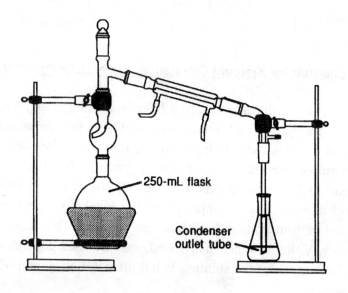

250-mL flask

Condenser outlet tube

Kjeldahl Distallation Apparatus

Titrate the ammonia in the distillate with 0.1 N HCl. The indicator color change is from blue to red with the endpoint taken when the last trace of blue has disappeared. Percent nitrogen is calculate by the equation:

$$\% \text{ N} = \frac{(\text{mL HCl sample} - \text{mL HCl blank})(\text{N HCl})(0.01401)}{(\text{g sample})} \times \frac{(100 \text{ mL of diluted digest})}{(90 \text{ mL of digest used})}$$

Laboratory and Lecture Demonstrations

General Discussion

The following lecture demonstrations have been used by the author to illustrate a variety of environmental principles. Some could potentially be used as laboratory experiments or as special student projects. Others are simply interesting applications of chemistry which relate to environmental chemistry.

Very brief introductory comments are given for each demonstration. The author assumes that the instructor will provide students with appropriate background information to relate the demonstration to course content. As always, appropriate eye protection and protective clothing should be worn.

1. Catalytic Oxidation of Acetone

This demonstration is used to illustrate heterogeneous catalysis. The chemistry is quite different from that involved in the automotive catalytic converter, but the principle of catalytic oxidation of a substance in the gaseous state is similar in both cases. Automotive catalytic converters use platinum to oxidize carbon monoxide and unburned hydrocarbons. Here copper is used to oxidize acetone vapor.

Apparatus and Procedure: A 250-mL beaker with steel wire gauze across the top of the beaker is set up with a small piece of copper screen wire mesh hanging from the wire gauze by means of a copper wire. A copper penny with a hole drilled in it and attached to the wire may be used, but the penny must be solid copper rather than a copper-clad zinc penny (the zinc will melt). U.S. pennies produced prior to about 1980 should be okay.

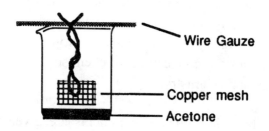

The copper mesh should be suspended so that it is about one-half inch above the liquid acetone. Remove the wire gauze and copper mesh from the beaker and heat the copper mesh in a burner flame until it glows red. Over-heating will cause the copper to melt, so be careful. Quickly return the copper mesh and wire gauze to the beaker. The glowing copper will begin oxidizing acetone vapor and will continue to glow red from the heat of reaction at the copper surface. This oxidation process will continue as long as acetone remains in the beaker. Remove the copper from the beaker and the glowing will cease.

2. Methane Density and Flammability

Methane, readily produced during anaerobic decay of organic matter and the major component of natural gas, has a density about half that of air. The following demonstration illustrates its low density and flammability.

Apparatus and Procedure: Connect a length of flexible tubing from a natural gas jet (source of methane) to a conical funnel. Put a pinch clamp on the flexible tubing so that the flow of gas can be controlled while holding the funnel. Turn on the gas at the gas jet. Dip the funnel in a beaker of soap solution or commercial "Bubble Stuff". Remove the funnel and use the pinch clamp to gently allow methane to produce a bubble at the end of the funnel. Shake the funnel gently to cause the bubble to break away from the funnel. It should float upward.

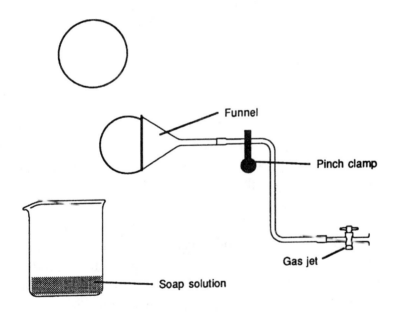

With the assistance of another person, use a lighted match to ignite one of the bubbles as it floats upward. It will burn with a gentle yellow flame. Be careful to keep face, hair and other body parts away from the bubble as it is ignited.

3. Gases that are Denser than Air: Petroleum Ether and CO_2

This demonstration is used to illustrate the heavier-than-air nature of several gases. One is flammable and the other is not. The dangers associated with the dangers of hydrocarbon vapors "crawling" along the floor and being ignited by matches, cigarettes, pilot lights, etc. can be discussed.

Apparatus and Procedure: Add 5-10 drops of petroleum ether (hexanes or heptane can also be used) to a 250-mL beaker and cover with a watch glass for a few minutes. "Pour" vapor but no liquid from the beaker into an empty 150-mL beaker. Hold the 250-mL beaker just above the smaller one and pour for about 15 seconds. Move the larger beaker containing the small amount of liquid safely away from the smaller beaker. Hold a lighted match just inside the 150-mL beaker. The vapor should ignite and burn gently down to the bottom of the beaker.

To another 250-mL beaker add a few pieces of dry ice (solid carbon dioxide) and cover with a watch glass for a few minutes. Pour carbon dioxide vapor into a 250-mL beaker. Lower a lighted match into the 150-mL beaker. The fire will be extinguished. The same match may be lowered into the beaker before adding the CO_2 to illustrate that the match is not extinguished until the carbon dioxide is added.

4. Tyndall Effect

The Tyndall effect is the "searchlight" effect observed when an intense beam of light is passed through a colloidal suspension. When viewed from the side, the beam can be seen because colloidal particles disperse the collimated light in all directions. The observation of automobile headlights piercing through fog is a good example of the Tyndall effect.

Apparatus and Procedure: Fill a large beaker (800-mL or 1000-mL) with slightly turbid or muddy water. Pass the light beam from a high-intensity microscope lamp or simply from a small bright flashlight that happens to have a fairly focused beam through the mixture in the beaker. With the room lights dimmed, the light beam (viewed at a right angle to the direction of the beam) can be seen piercing through the suspension. A colloidal suspension can also be easily generated by filling the beaker with water and adding a few drops of milk. Air made cloudy with cigarette smoke will also exhibit the Tyndall effect.

This principle can be used to illustrate the effectiveness of alum treatment of muddy water and of electrostatic precipitation of particulates suspended in the air.

5. Alum Treatment of Muddy Water

Drinking water or wastewater is sometimes treated with lime and alum to aid in the precipitation of suspended particles. This demonstration simply and quickly show the effect of such treatment. The reaction is:

$$2KAl(SO_4)_2(aq) + 3Ca(OH)_2(aq) \longrightarrow Al(OH)_3(s) + CaSO_4(s) + K_2SO$$

As the gelatinous aluminum hydroxide, $Al(OH)_3$, precipitate forms, suspended particles of mud and silt are trapped by the precipitate. The aluminum hydroxide settles and carries particles that cause turbidity with it. The turbidity, which would have required many hours or even days to be removed, is greatly reduced in about 15 minutes.

Apparatus and Procedure: Fill an 800-mL beaker with about 600 mL muddy water. Add 10-20 grams of granular alum, (potassium aluminum sulfate, $KAl(SO_4)_2$), and stir to dissolve. Normally, a limewater solution (saturated $Ca(OH)_2$) is added to provide the hydroxide ion concentration needed to form aluminum hydroxide. However, the same result can be obtained by adding 5 mL of 14 M aqueous ammonia with stirring. Aluminum hydroxide is amphoteric and will dissolve if the hydroxide concentration becomes too great. Aqueous ammonia is a sufficiently weak base that aluminum hydroxide will not dissolve if too much is added.

If a flocculent, gelatinous precipitate is not observed within a minute of adding the aqueous ammonia, add about 5 more milliliters. The precipitate should settle, carrying most turbidity with it, within 15 to 30 minutes. Compare the Tyndall effect produced by untreated and treated water samples. Note the color of the precipitate. If mud particles were not present, the precipitate would be white.

6. Electrostatic Precipitation of Smoke Particulates

The electrostatic precipitator (Cottrell Precipitator) is a highly efficient method for removing particulate matter from the air. Colloidally dispersed smoke particles carry a static electrical charge which causes them to repel one another thereby preventing them from coagulating and settling from the air.

The electrostatic precipitator uses high-voltage direct current to attract charged colloidal particles to a surface of opposite charge. Particles are removed rapidly and with efficiencies of greater than 99%.

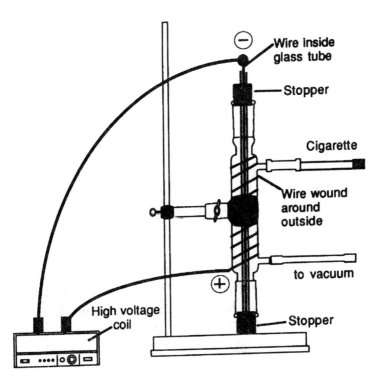

Apparatus and Procedure: The electrostatic precipitator is constructed from the outer jacket of a 2-piece condenser. *Note*: The inner glass tube must be made from ordinary laboratory soft-glass or borosilicate tubing (sealed at the bottom end) *and must be* held in place with a 1-hole rubber stopper at each end of the condenser jacket. It is a good idea to insert the bottom (closed) end of the tube just enough into the lower stopper so that it seals the hole but so that it can be easily disconnected later. Wrap 1 to 2 meters of copper wire around the outside of the condenser jacket and fasten at the top and bottom with tape or adhesive. Leave a little wire extending away from the condenser so that an alligator clip can be attached to it. Run a heavier gauge wire (14 or 16 gauge) through the center tube and make a loop at the top so that an alligator clip can be attached to it. Connect the negative lead from a high-voltage (10,000 volts) DC coil to the wire running down the center of the unit. Connect the positive lead from the coil to the wire wrapped around the outside of the jacket.

Use a vacuum source (this may be as simple as a squeeze bulb or a syringe) to draw smoke from the lighted cigarette into the unit. Turn on the high voltage coil. The cloudiness should disappear immediately. *Be careful to avoid being zapped by a spark from the coil!* While the coil is operating, more smoke may be drawn into the apparatus. It will "disappear" as fast as it enters the system. After the particulate matter from half a cigarette or so has been precipitated, the unit may be disconnected from the electricity source and the center glass tube removed. Because cigarette smoke particles or oil droplets tend to be positively charge, most of the brown "tar" will have precipitated on the negatively charged center rod. Wiping it with a tissue or paper towel will demonstrate the oily nature of this particulate matter.

7. Surface Tension and Lowering it with a Surfactant

Various objects that are more dense than water can be made to float if carefully placed on the surface of water so that the object is suspended by the water's surface tension. The objects will sink if enough downward force is applied to break the surface tension or if a surfactant is added to lower the surface tension.

Apparatus and Procedure: Use laboratory distilled or deionized water. If "hard" tap water is used, it is likely to reduce the effectiveness of certain surfactants. Try floating a pin on the water by using a forceps and gently setting the *dry* object on the surface. Strawberry baskets (1-pint) constructed from plastic mesh are easy to place on the surface of a container of water. The basket is held up by the water's surface structure. Alternatively, a basket can be constructed from aluminum or copper window screen mesh. The basket is constructed by cutting and folding as shown below with the bottom being a few inches on each edge. The students or instructor may experiment with various sizes and shapes.

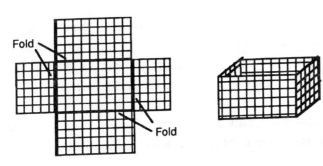

Once the object is floating, addition of a surfactant should cause it to sink. Usually, the addition of just one drop of a dilute dish or laundry detergent solution will be sufficient to cause the object to sink, but sometimes several drops are needed. Soap and detergent solutions all have the ability to reduce the surface tension of water. Again, a good deal of experimentation can be done with different kinds of soaps and detergents and with soft water, hard water, and distilled or deionized water.

8. Bielstein Copper Wire Test for Halogenated Organics

A classic organic qualitative test for the presence or absence of a halogen in an organic molecule is the copper-wire test. This test has several environmental applications. In most labs these days, we have waste containers for both halogenated and non-halogenated organic solvents. If there is ever a question as to whether an unknown solvent is halogenated, the Bielstein test is quick and sensitive. It can also be used to test plastic films and bottles. For example, polyvinyl chloride (PVC) and polyvinylidene chloride (Saran) will give nice positive tests, but polyethylene will yield a negative test. Finally, this test might be used to determine whether a transformer oil is a polychlorinated biphenyl (PCB).

The Bielstein test is very sensitive and generally does not produce false negative results. It may produce a false positive if halogen traces are present or if a previous sample has not been thoroughly cleaned from the wire.

Apparatus and Procedure: Push a 5-inch length of 14- or 16-gauge copper wire into a cork so that the wire is held firmly by the cork. The cork serves as a handle so that the hot wire can be held by hand without being burned. A small loop should be bent into the end of the wire so that it will hold a drop of liquid solvent.

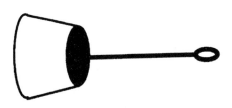

Hold the looped end of the wire in a burner flame long enough to burn off any salts from perspiration and other contamination. The wire may be heated to a dull red, but more intense heating will cause the wire to melt.

After contaminants have been burned from the wire, dip it in the liquid to be tested and withdraw a drop of liquid in the wire loop. Put the wire in the flame. If a halogen is present (Cl, Br, or I) the wire will impart a green color to the flame. Absence of green coloration indicates the absence of halogens.

For polymers, heat the wire and touch the hot wire to the plastic to be tested so that some of the polymer melts on the wire. Put the wire in the flame. A green or blue-green flame color is a positive test. The fluorocarbon, Teflon®, does not produce a positive test.

Between samples the wire should be heated thoroughly to remove traces from previous samples.

9. Disappearing Polystyrene Popcorn

Polystyrene (styrofoam) packing popcorn is commonly used to protect packages from damage during transportation. Styrofoam products represent a waste disposal problem because they take up a great deal of landfill space.

This demonstration appears quite magical because a dozen or more cups full of the popcorn can be added to a single cup of similar size with all the material sinking into the cup always leaving room for more.

This demonstration can be used to discuss the value of recycling and the pros and cons of using a technique like the one involved here to aid with recycling.

Apparatus and Procedure: Fill a coffee mug about one-fourth full with acetone. Use another similarly sized mug to transfer polystyrene packing popcorn to the acetone-containing cup. With a little shaking or stirring, the polystyrene sinks into the cup and appears to disappear. Ten or more cups full can be added to the acetone-containing cup with the popcorn disappearing just as fast as ever.

The polystyrene softens and becomes a viscous syrup in the bottom of the cup. After quite a bit of polystyrene has been added, the acetone may be decanted into a waste container and the viscous polystyrene poured onto a paper towel. If allowed to stand on the towel over night, the acetone will evaporate leaving a solid chunk of plastic.

218

Packing popcorn made from starch rather than polystyrene will not work. However, water will soften the starch popcorn, but not as dramatically as the effect of acetone on polystyrene.

10. Combustion of Aliphatic and Aromatic Hydrocarbons and Alcohols

Aliphatic hydrocarbons tend to burn more cleanly than aromatic hydrocarbons. Although this qualitative test for aromatic structure is very crude, it illustrates the fact that fuels containing high percentages of toluene, xylenes, etc. burn less cleanly than fuels containing only aliphatic hydrocarbons. Alcohols burn most cleanly, and ethanol is currently being used up to 10% in most gasolines. The cleaner burning reformulated gasolines (RFG) that are currently on the market contain the two alcohols ethanol and methanol as well as two other "oxygenates" ethyl-tert-butyl ether (ETBE) and methyl-tert-butyl ether (MTBE).

Apparatus and Procedure: Place a watch glass on the desk top. From a dropping bottle add one or two drops of an aliphatic hydrocarbon, such as heptane, octane, or petroleum ether, to the center of the watch glass. Ignite the liquid with a match. Note the yellow flame with relatively little black smoke.

Repeat the above procedure using toluene or xylene(s). The hydrocarbon should burn with a great deal of black smoke visible even from fairly far away.

Also, repeat the procedure with ethanol or methanol. These alcohols burn visibly cleaner than either aliphatic or aromatic hydrocarbons.

11. Explosive Behavior of Ethanol

Although ethanol burns cleaner than the hydrocarbons found in gasoline, its vapor can burn with explosive speed when mixed with air in the correct fuel/air mixture.

Apparatus and Procedure: Polyethylene bottles ranging in size from 250 mL to 1000 mL may be used to build the "alcohol cannon" shown below. Fasten sheet-rock screws into opposite sides of each bottle used so that a gap of about one-fourth inch exists between the tips of the two screws. We generally use three bottles: a 250-mL, a 500-mL, and a 1-L .

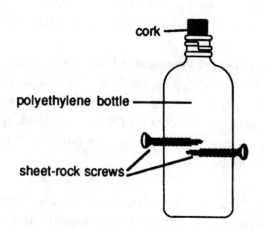

Pour 5 to 10 mL of absolute ethanol into each bottle, put a cork (not a rubber stopper) in the opening of the bottle and shake to cause the ethanol to vaporize. Hold the tip of an operating Tesla coil near the part of one of the sheet-rock screws extending outside the bottle so that a spark jumps from the Tesla coil to the end of the screw. This should cause a spark to jump the gap inside the bottle igniting the alcohol vapor and shooting the cork out of the bottles with explosive force. Corks work fine because they do little damage to the ceiling. Rubber stoppers are too dangerous and should not be used.

APPENDIX

A. CONSTANTS AND EQUATIONS

1 cal = 4.184 J

$1 \text{ J} = 9.48 \times 10^{-4}$ Btu

2.2 lb = 1 kg   1 lb = 453.6 g

The gas constant is 0.082 L • atm/K • mol

Avogadro's number = 6.02×10^{23}

1 m = 39.37 in

$1 \text{ m}^3 = 1000 \text{ L}$

$$1 \text{ atm} = 1.013 \times 10^5 \text{ Pa}$$
$$= 29.92 \text{ in Hg}$$
$$= 760 \text{ mm Hg}$$
$$= 14.7 \text{ lb/in}^2$$

1 mg/L = 1 µg/mL = 1 ng/µL $\cong$ 1 ppm (dil. aq. solution)

E = hc/λ and E = hν

h = 6.626×10^{-27} erg sec = Planck's constant

c = 3.0×108 m/s = speed of light

B. PREFIXES FOR METRIC AND SI UNITS

Prefix	*Abbreviation*	*Multiplication Factor*
tera	T	10^{12}
giga	G	10^{9}
mega	M	10^{6}
kilo	k	10^{3}
hecto	h	10^{2}
deka	da	10^{1}
deci	d	10^{-1}
centi	c	10^{-2}
milli	m	10^{-3}
micro	μ	10^{-6}
nano	n	10^{-9}
pico	p	10^{-12}
femto	f	10^{-15}
atto	a	10^{-18}

C. COMMON IONS

POSITIVE IONS

One Positive Charge

NH_4^+	Ammonium
Cu^+	Copper(I) (cuprous)
H^+	Hydrogen
K^+	Potassium
Ag^+	Silver
Na^+	Sodium

Two Positive Charges

Ba^{2+}	Barium
Ca^{2+}	Calcium
Co^{2+}	Cobalt
Cu^{2+}	Copper(II) (cupric)
Fe^{2+}	Iron(II) (ferrous)
Hg_2^{2+}	Mercury(I) (mercurous)
Pb^{2+}	Lead(II) (plumbous)
Mg^{2+}	Magnesium
Hg^{2+}	Mercury(II) (mercuric)
Sn^{2+}	Tin(II) (stannous)
Zn^{2+}	Zinc

Three Positive Charges

Al^{3+}	Aluminum
As^{3+}	Arsenic(III) (arsenious)
Bi^{3+}	Bismuth
Cr^{3+}	Chromium(III) (chromic)
Fe^{3+}	Iron(III) (ferric)

Four Positive Charges

Sn^{4+}	Tin(IV) (stannic)
Pb^{4+}	Lead(IV) (plumbic)

Five Positive Charges

As^{5+}	Arsenic(V) (arsenic)
Sb^{5+}	Antimony V (antimonic)

NEGATIVE IONS

One Negative Charge

$C_2H_3O_2^-$	Acetate
Br^-	Bromide
ClO_3^-	Chlorate
Cl^-	Chloride
CN^-	Cyanide
F^-	Fluoride
HCO_3^-	Hydrogen Carbonate (bicarbonate)
OH^-	Hydroxide
I^-	Iodide
NO_3^-	Nitrate
NO_2^-	Nitrite
MnO_4^-	Permanganate

Two Negative Charges

CO_3^{2-}	Carbonate
CrO_4^{2-}	Chromate
$Cr_2O_7^{2-}$	Dichromate
O^{2-}	Oxide
SO_4^{2-}	Sulfate
S^{2-}	Sulfide
SO_3^{2-}	Sulfite
$C_2O_4^{2-}$	Oxalate

Three Negative Charges

AsO_4^{3-}	Arsenate
AsO_3^{3-}	Arsenite
PO_4^{3-}	Phosphate
$Fe(CN)_6^{3-}$	Ferricyanide

D. GREEK ALPHABET

Greek Letter		*Name*	*Keyboard letter*
α	A	alpha	A
β	B	beta	B
γ	Γ	gamma	G
δ	Δ	delta	D
ε	E	epsilon	E
ζ	Z	zeta	Z
η	H	eta	H
θ	Θ	theta	Q
ι	I	iota	I
κ	K	kappa	K
λ	Λ	lambda	L
μ	M	mu	M
ν	N	nu	N
ξ	Ξ	xi	X
o	O	omicron	O
π	Π	pi	P
ρ	P	rho	R
σ	Σ	sigma	S
τ	T	tau	T
υ	Y	upsilon	U
φ	Φ	phi	F
χ	X	chi	C
ψ	Ψ	psi	Y
ω	Ω	omega	W

E. GREEK LETTERS IN ENVIRONMENTAL CHEMISTRY

α, β, γ, and δ may be used to represent the position of substituents on complex organic molecules such as benzo-(α)pyrene.

δ is often used to mean "partial".

Ω is a unit of electrical resistance (the ohm).

℧ is a unit of electrical conductivity (the mho).

σ often represents "standard deviation".

Δ usually means "change in" or "difference between".

Σ usually means "sum".

Π usually means "product of ".

μ is a metric prefix meaning "micro" or "one one-millionth of ".

ν symbolizes light or sound frequency often in units of Hertz (Hz).

η symbolizes viscosity in poise (dyn sec cm^{-2}).

γ symbolizes surface tension in dyn cm^{-1}.

λ symbolizes light or sound wavelength in nm, cm, m, etc.

α and β are symbols for subatomic particles produced by radioisotopes.

γ is often used to represent high energy gamma radiation produced by radioisotopes or found in cosmic rays.

π is 3.14159....

F. ABBREVIATIONS

angstrom	Å
atmosphere	atm
atomic mass unit	amu
British thermal unit	Btu
calorie	cal
curie	Ci
degree Celsius	°C
degree Fahrenheit	°F
Kelvins	K
hertz	H
joule	J
molal	m
molar	M
mole	mol
ohm	Ω
parts per million	ppm
torricelli	torr
volt	V or v
watt	W or w
mean or average	$\bar{x}$

G. SUGGESTIONS FOR KEEPING A LABORATORY NOTEBOOK

The laboratory notebook is your record of what you have done in the lab. It should be sufficiently complete so that you can reproduce the experiment at another time if necessary.

Several pages at the beginning of the book should be left blank for a table of contents. Written notes should be kept <u>only</u> on the right hand page. The left or back of each page should not be used. The following sections should be included in the recording of data for each experiment.

1. Description of experiment
   a. objective
   b. method used
      • solution and sample preparation
      • glassware used
      • balances
      • dilutions
      • etc.

2. Data... Try to record in the form of tables. Graphs produced by instruments or plots made with a computer should be trimmed to fit a notebook page and taped or stapled in place in the notebook.

3. Calculations... Again, try to use tables whenever possible.

4. Results and Discussion... Discuss the results and whether they make sense.

5. Error Analysis... Discuss errors you may have made and other errors that you think are built into the procedure.

H. PERIODIC TABLE OF ELEMENTS

IA (1)	IIA (2)	IIIA (3)	IVA (4)	VA (5)	VIA (6)	VIIA (7)	(8)	VIIIA (9)	(10)	IB (11)	IIB (12)	IIIB (13)	VB (14)	VB (15)	VIB (16)	VIIB (17)	VIIIa (18)
1 H 1.01																	2 He 4.00
3 Li 6.94	4 Be 9.01											5 B 10.8	6 C 12.0	7 N 14.0	8 O 16.0	9 F 19.0	10 Ne 20.2
11 Na 23.0	12 Mg 24.3											13 Al 27.0	14 Si 28.1	15 P 31.0	16 S 32.1	17 Cl 35.5	18 Ar 39.9
19 K 39.1	20 Ca 40.1	21 Sc 45.0	22 Ti 48.0	23 V 50.9	24 Cr 52.0	25 Mn 54.9	26 Fe 55.8	27 Co 58.9	28 Ni 58.7	29 Cu 63.5	30 Zn 65.4	31 Ga 69.7	32 Ge 72.6	33 As 74.9	34 Se 79.0	35 Br 79.9	36 Kr 83.8
37 Rb 85.5	38 Sr 87.6	39 Y 88.9	40 Zr 91.2	41 Nb 92.9	42 Mo 95.9	43 Tc (98)	44 Ru 101	45 Rh 103	46 Pd 106	47 Ag 108	48 Cd 112	49 In 115	50 Sn 119	51 Sb 122	52 Te 128	53 I 127	54 Xe 131
55 Cs 133	56 Ba 137	57 La 139	72 Hf 178	73 Ta 181	74 W 184	75 Re 186	76 Os 190	77 Ir 192	78 Pt 195	79 Au 197	80 Hg 201	81 Tl 204	82 Pb 207	83 Bi 209	84 Po (209)	85 At (210)	86 Rn (222)
87 Fr (223)	88 Ra 226	89 Ac 227															

58 Ce 140	59 Pr 141	60 Nd 144	61 Pm (145)	62 Sm 150	63 Eu 152	64 Gd 157	65 Tb 159	66 Dy 163	67 Ho 165	68 Er 167	69 Tm 169	70 Yb 173	71 Lu 175
90 Th 232	91 Pa 231	92 U 238	93 Np 237	94 Pu (244)	95 Am (243)	96 Cm (247)	97 Bk (247)	98 Cf (251)	99 Es (252)	100 Fm (257)	101 Md (258)	102 No (259)	103 Lr (260)